Consumer Finance Risk Monitor

OECD

BETTER POLICIES FOR BETTER LIVES

Please cite this publication as:
OECD (2024), *Consumer Finance Risk Monitor*, OECD Publishing, Paris, https://doi.org/10.1787/047b2ea6-en.

ISBN 978-92-64-55168-8 (print)
ISBN 978-92-64-37647-2 (pdf)
ISBN 978-92-64-31988-2 (HTML)
ISBN 978-92-64-95219-5 (epub)

Photo credits: cover © whyframestudio/ Getty Images

Corrigenda to OECD publications may be found on line at: www.oecd.org/about/publishing/corrigenda.htm.

Foreword

The OECD Consumer Finance Risk Monitor provides an analysis of risks facing financial consumers globally. It analyses consumer harm and complaints in five product markets (banking and payments, credit, insurance, investments and pensions) and describes regulatory and supervisory responses to address market conduct risks. It also highlights tools used to monitor risks and presents data on financial scams and frauds.

The report was prepared by the Financial Consumer Protection, Education and Inclusion Unit in the Capital Markets and Financial Institutions Division of the OECD Directorate for Financial and Enterprise Affairs. The report benefited from the contributions of national government delegates, particularly delegates to the G20/OECD Task Force on Financial Consumer Protection.

It also benefited from inputs from members of the Consumer Finance Risk Monitor Working Group: David Pereira, Banco de Portugal; Juan Carlos Izaguirre, Olga Tomilova and Eric Duflos, CGAP; Nadia Linciano and Monica Gentile, CONSOB (Italy); Marco Traversa and Giacomo Barbet, EIOPA; Sam Stoakes, FCA (UK); Juanita Smit and Marrelie Victor, FSCA (South Africa); Miguel Rivera Melgar, Paola Tamayo Medrano and Luis Daniel Allain Cañote, SBS (Peru).

The report was prepared by Matthew Soursourian and Rachel Karen, under the oversight of Miles Larbey. Editorial and communication support was provided by Eva Abbott and Meral Gedik. Sally Day-Hanotiaux provided support to the project.

The Monitor will inform the priorities of the G20/OECD Task Force on Financial Consumer Protection and contribute toward the development of policy guidance by providing evidence related to the risks facing financial consumers. Policymakers, public authorities and other stakeholders can draw upon the Monitor to inform legal and regulatory reform to enhance financial consumer protection where required, guide market monitoring and effectively address consumer detriment. The Monitor will inform the development of the Programme of Work for the G20/OECD Task Force on Financial Consumer Protection, including future areas of research and analysis, roundtable discussions and seminars, and the development of policy guidance.

Table of contents

FIGURES

INFOGRAPHICS

TABLES

BOXES

Follow OECD Publications on:

https://twitter.com/OECD

https://www.facebook.com/theOECD

https://www.linkedin.com/company/organisation-eco-cooperation-development-organisation-cooperation-developpement-eco/

https://www.youtube.com/user/OECDiLibrary

https://www.oecd.org/newsletters/

Executive summary

Consumers of financial products and services face a complex landscape with a range of evolving issues, opportunities and risks. In this context, it is critical for policymakers, national authorities and international bodies responsible for financial consumer protection to identify and monitor the risks affecting financial consumers, track consumer detriment and share effective approaches that can help address these risks and harms. The Consumer Finance Risk Monitor (the Monitor), developed by the G20/OECD Task Force on Financial Consumer Protection, synthesises the perspectives of 43 jurisdictions on risks to financial consumers in 2022 and 2023. The Monitor covers current and emerging risks stemming from the operating environment; demand-side risks; conduct-related risks; tools used to monitor risks; products and services giving rise to consumer detriment; consumer complaints; and financial scams and frauds. To address risks to financial consumers, policymakers should ensure the full implementation of comprehensive financial consumer protection frameworks in line with the G20/OECD High-Level Principles of Financial Consumer Protection to strengthen supervisory capacity, empower financial consumers and protect those who may be vulnerable.

Key risks include inflation and rising interest rates, financial scams and frauds, and poor-value products and services

Jurisdictions identified key risks to financial consumers in three broad categories: conduct-related risks, demand-side risks, and risk stemming from the operating environment. In most cases, it was anticipated that the significance of these risks would remain the same, or increase in 2023.

The most significant risks arising from the conduct of financial institutions include poor-value financial products and services, ineffective disclosures and dishonest sales practices.

The most significant risks related to the characteristics and circumstances of consumers (demand-side risks) include a lack of financial literacy, over-indebtedness and a lack of digital capability. More broadly, jurisdictions shared concerns relating to various forms of consumer vulnerability.

The most significant risks stemming from the broader operating environment include inflation and rising interest rates, financial scams and frauds, and new business models and digital innovation.

The following areas also emerged as significant risks: increasing incidence and complexity of scams and frauds; new credit products and risk of over-indebtedness; innovation in digital technology and business models; increasing access to crypto-assets, which may be unregulated in some jurisdictions or issued and traded in a manner not compliant with applicable domestic regulations in others; alternative sources of financial advice; and greenwashing and other risks linked to sustainable finance.

Financial scams and frauds rose in most jurisdictions, accelerated by digitalisation

Financial scams and frauds continue to be a major concern among jurisdictions. Most jurisdictions (72%) noted that the reported incidence of financial scams and frauds increased in 2022 compared to 2021. In jurisdictions where data are available, the total amount of financial losses due to scams and frauds also increased from 2021 to 2022. This growth in financial losses ranged from a 5% increase in Singapore to a 79% increase in Australia. The most common types of scams and frauds by number of people affected were tricking consumers into providing personal identification information and fake schemes designed to tempt consumers to transfer, pay or invest money or buy fake insurance.

The total volume of consumer complaints increased in most reporting jurisdictions in 2022

Data gathered through consumer complaints about financial products and services can signal gaps in financial consumer protection frameworks and highlight areas that may need to be addressed by policymakers and regulatory and supervisory authorities tasked with administering and enforcing financial consumer protection laws, regulations and other measures. In around three quarters of responding jurisdictions, complaints filed directly with firms or with alternative dispute resolution mechanisms increased from 2021 to 2022. Complaints filed with supervisory authorities also increased in more than half of responding jurisdictions.

Monitoring consumer detriment from financial products can help policymakers identify and address areas of concern

Transaction accounts, debit cards, mobile banking and digital wallets gave rise to the greatest consumer detriment in the banking and payments sector, primarily due to harms linked to financial scams and frauds and blocked accounts. Detriment arising from these products was expected to increase in 2023 as inadequately regulated digitalisation may increase consumers' exposure to scams and frauds.

Mortgages and home loans gave rise to the greatest consumer detriment in the credit sector in 2022, primarily due to interest rate hikes and cost of living increases that, while not necessarily the result of misconduct by financial services providers, still negatively affected consumers' budgets.

Motor and life insurance gave rise to the greatest consumer detriment in the insurance sector in 2022. Jurisdictions noted that certain business practices in the sector, such as bundling or tying products, risk causing consumer detriment in the absence of effective disclosures and transparency. Authorities also reported confusion among consumers about insurance coverage and dissatisfaction with claims handling and compensation.

Crypto-assets gave rise to the greatest consumer detriment in the investments sector. Jurisdictions expected that the harm from crypto-assets would increase in 2023 along with detriment from self-directed investments, equity and sustainable financial products.

Benefits payments and management of assets gave rise to the greatest consumer detriment in the pensions sector in 2022, in part linked to volatility in financial markets in 2021/22 that caused the performance of some pension funds to deteriorate. In addition, jurisdictions noted that detriment arose from commission structures that create incentives for distributors to persuade consumers to purchase products with high commissions, even if they are not in line with outcome expectations and risk appetites.

Effective approaches to address current and emerging risks include comprehensive financial consumer protection frameworks, strengthening supervisory capacity and empowering consumers

Jurisdictions have undertaken and planned a range of initiatives to address current and emerging risks. Effective approaches start from the basis of implementing and improving comprehensive financial consumer protection frameworks in line with the G20/OECD High-Level Principles of Financial Consumer Protection, the leading international standard for effective and comprehensive financial consumer protection frameworks. In addition, addressing consumer-facing risks requires strengthening supervisory capacity, empowering financial consumers and paying special attention to consumers who may be vulnerable.

1 Monitoring risks faced by financial consumers

Consumers of financial products and services are confronted by a complex and varied landscape that presents a range of evolving risks. In this context, it is critical for policymakers, national authorities and international forums to actively monitor the risks to financial consumers, track consumer detriment and share effective approaches that can help address these risks and harms. The G20/OECD Task Force on Financial Consumer Protection has developed the Consumer Finance Risk Monitor to support these objectives and facilitate global dialogue. This chapter provides an overview of recent economic and financial trends and describes the development and methodology of the Consumer Finance Risk Monitor.

1.1. Introduction

Consumers of financial products and services are confronted by a complex landscape with a range of evolving risks. These risks may stem from the broader economic context (i.e. risks arising from the operating environment), the characteristics and circumstances of consumers themselves (i.e. demand-side risks) or from the behaviour and actions of financial services providers (i.e. conduct risks). While recovering from the effects of a global pandemic, consumers around the world are facing ongoing supply chain crises, armed conflicts and natural disasters. At the same time, high inflation and elevated interest rates result in an increase of borrowing costs and erode consumer's purchasing power and the real value of their savings and investments. Alongside a rising incidence of financial scams and frauds, new business models and innovations are making riskier products more accessible. These risks are compounded by a lack of financial and digital capabilities, over-indebtedness and insufficient income. And while financial products and services have the potential to mitigate these risks and support the financial well-being of consumers, the conduct of financial services providers can exacerbate the vulnerability of consumers and destabilise their financial situations. Poor value financial products and services, ineffective disclosures, poor financial advice and dishonest sales practices comprise key risks faced by financial consumers in their dealings with firms.

In this context, it is critical for policymakers, national authorities and international forums to monitor the risks to financial consumers, track consumer detriment and share effective approaches that can help address these risks and harms. The G20/OECD Task Force on Financial Consumer Protection has developed the Consumer Finance Risk Monitor (the Monitor) to support these objectives and facilitate global dialogue. This publication synthesises the perspectives of 43 jurisdictions on risks facing financial consumers, focusing on the calendar year 2022.

1.2. Recent economic and financial trends

Nearly four years after the start of the COVID-19 pandemic, economic recovery around the globe remained uneven.[1] The pandemic's significant impact on the global economy and labour markets highlighted inequalities, with many of the most vulnerable citizens of society worst affected. Especially in emerging market economies, experts foresaw that the pandemic would lead to *economic scarring,* defined by the International Monetary Fund as "diminished long-term output relative to pre-pandemic projections", due to the pandemic's adverse effects on capital, labour and overall productivity (International Monetary Fund, 2022[1]). Disruptions to schooling, for instance, led to learning losses that disproportionally affected poorer students. If unaddressed, these learning losses will diminish human capital and productivity in the coming decades.

One of the key continuing challenges as the global economy grappled with these longer-term effects of the pandemic was addressing supply chain issues so that goods and services continue to reach consumers.

In parallel, the war in Ukraine drove rising inflation, increasing prices of many common goods and services used by consumers around the globe. Given the effects of the war and ongoing impact of COVID-19, in June 2022 the OECD revised its economic projections downward, predicting global growth for 2022 to be around 3.0% (down from the 4.5% rate that had been estimated in December 2021). As of 2023, the OECD estimated that the global economy had grown by 3.3% in 2022 (OECD, 2023[2]), with a growth rate predicted of 3.0% in 2023 and 2.7% in 2024 (OECD, 2023[3]). As shown in Figure 1.1, annual inflation rates in 2023 remained elevated across global regions, most notably in Latin America and the Caribbean (13.8%), Middle East and Central Asia (18%), and Sub-Saharan Africa (15.8%) (International Monetary Fund, 2023[4]).

Figure 1.1. Annual inflation rate, by region, 2023

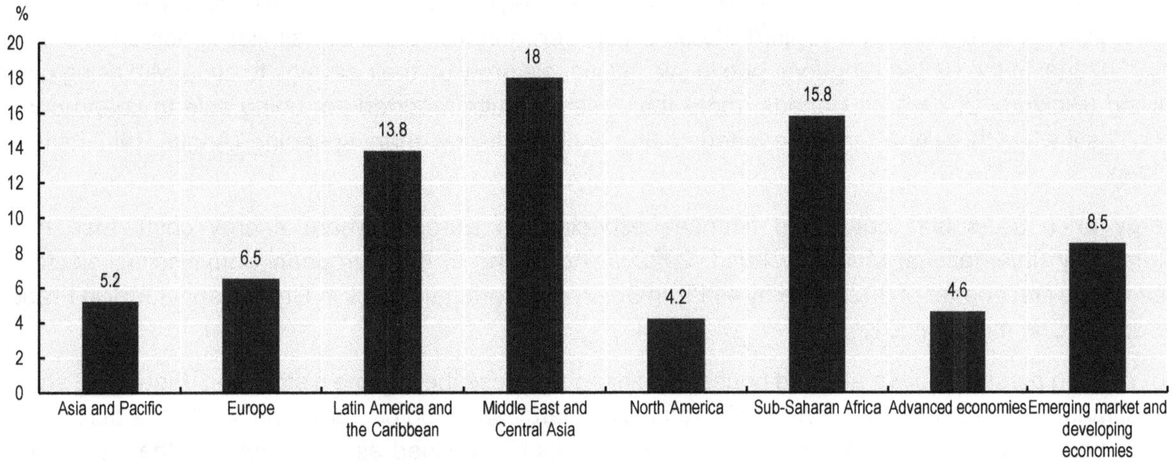

Source: IMF World Economic Outlook, October 2023.

Inflation pressures also prompted many central banks to start increasing their monetary policy rates and, in several cases, unwinding their asset purchasing programmes. As shown in Figure 1.2, these increases from 2020 to 2023 varied significantly across jurisdictions, and included no changes (e.g. Japan), increases from a base rate of zero or close to zero (e.g. Australia, Canada, euro area, Peru, United Kingdom and United States) as well as significant hikes of 1 000 basis points or more (e.g. Brazil, Colombia).

Figure 1.2. Central bank policy rates, 2020 and 2023

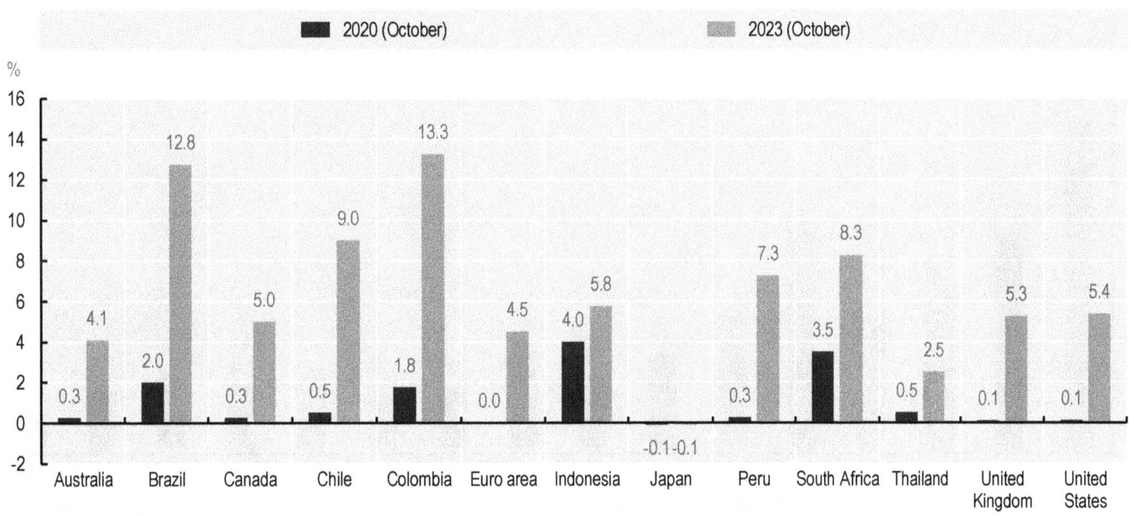

Note: Data corresponds to rates on 31 October 2020 and 31 October 2023.
Source: Bank for International Settlements – BIS Policy Rate Statistics.

Inflation pressures, rising costs of goods and services, and increases in interest rates all contributed to a cost-of-living crisis that had a consequential impact on household finances and on households' risk of financial hardship. According to an analysis by Moody's Analytics, US households in 2022 were spending, on average, an extra USD 341 (United States dollar) per month to purchase similar goods and services (Fox, 2022[5]). In the United Kingdom, one in five individuals drew on their savings to cope with rising costs of living (Pickford, 2022[6]). In Canada, more than half of adults reported not being able to keep up with rising costs while three quarters of reported cutting back on discretionary spending (Angus Reid Institute, 2022[7]).

Energy price hikes hurt household finances especially in Europe, where energy costs rose most dramatically (International Monetary Fund, 2022[8]). According to the European Commission, electricity prices in the first quarter of 2022 rose by 411% in Spain and Portugal, 343% in Greece and 336% in France (European Commission, 2022[9]).

Cost of living pressures have affected household finances across the income distribution. Figure 1.3 shows the estimated impact of the year-on-year increases in energy and food prices in April 2022 as a percentage of total household expenditures. For low-income households, defined as households in the first income quintile, the cost increases of food and energy represent a greater proportion of their total household expenditures compared to high-income households, defined as households in the fifth quintile. As Figure 1.3 shows, while price increases affect household finances across the income distribution, they are most acutely felt by low-income households.

Figure 1.3. Cost increases of food and energy as a percentage of household expenditures in selected OECD countries, April 2022

Percentage increase in household expenditures for the lowest and highest income quintiles

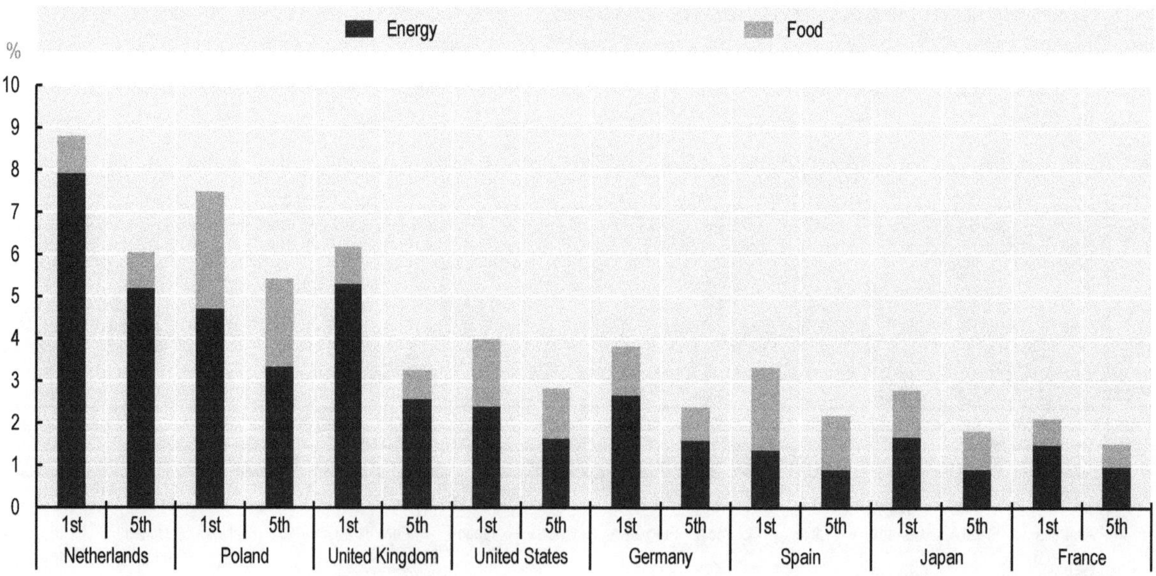

Source: Bureau of Economic Analysis, Statistics Bureau of Japan, Eurostat, and OECD calculations published in OECD (2023[2]), *OECD Economic Outlook, Volume 2023 Issue 1.*

At the same time, inflation undermines real wages, which puts further pressure on household finances and exacerbates the cost-of-living crisis. According to estimates from the United Nations, the average household lost approximately 1.5% in real income due to price increases in corn and wheat alone (United Nations, 2022[10]).

The percentage change in real wages from 2021 to 2022 in eight regions and twelve OECD countries are presented in Figure 1.4 and Figure 1.5 below. Households and individuals who might not have previously been considered vulnerable may have found themselves in a more precarious situation in 2022.

Figure 1.4. Annual average real wage growth by region, 2021 and 2022

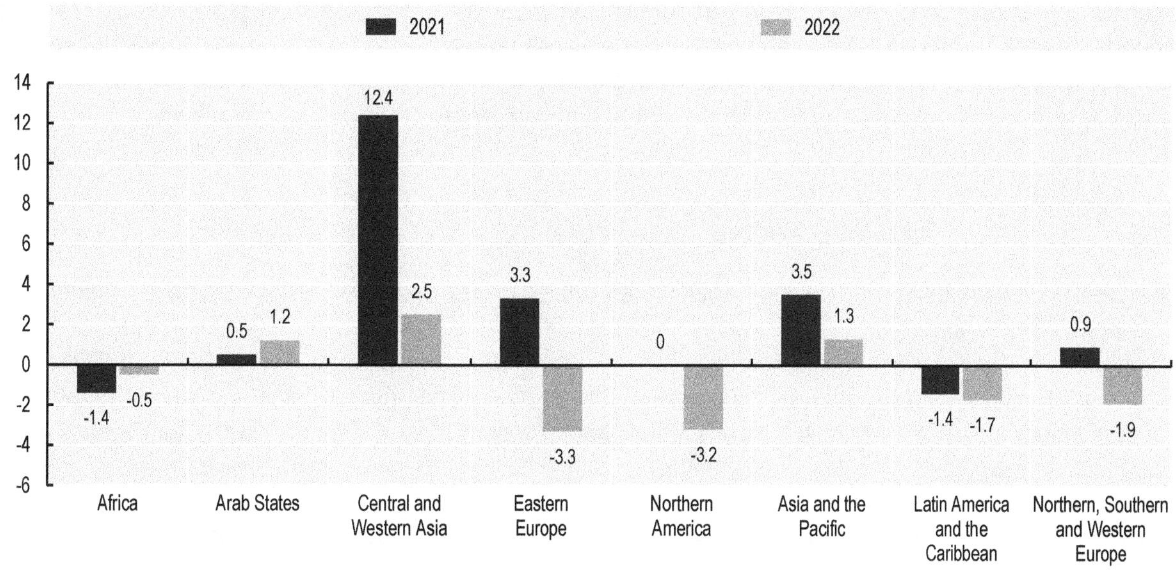

Source: ILO Global Wage Report 2022-23.

Figure 1.5. Percentage change in real wages in selected OECD countries, 2021 to 2022

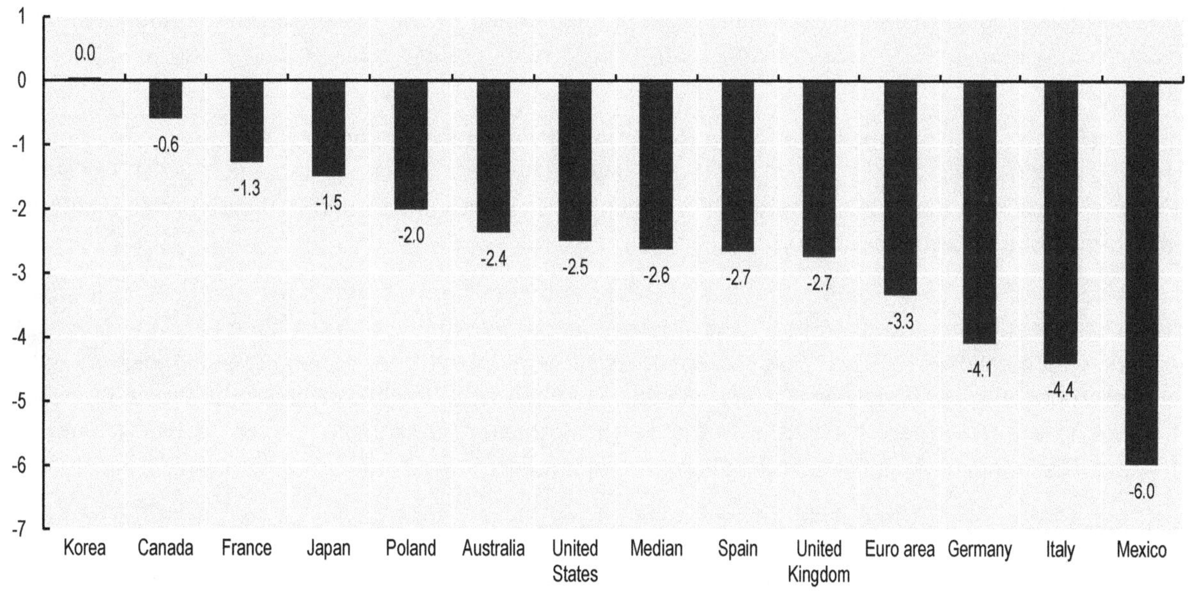

Note: Data is based on compensation per employee deflated by the personal consumption expenditures deflator. The median is the median of all available OECD countries.

Source: OECD Economic Outlook 113 database; Federal Reserve Bank of Atlanta; Indeed; Ministry of Health, Labour and Welfare of Japan; Statistics Canada; Office for National Statistics; and OECD calculations, published in OECD (2023[2]), *OECD Economic Outlook, Volume 2023 Issue 1*.

The impact of these financial and economic trends on households is evident in demographic research. In the most recent edition of the OECD Risks That Matter (RTM) Survey, conducted biennially since 2018, personal finance was a top concern for responding individuals, and these worries appear to be growing over time (OECD, 2023[11]). Across the 27 000 individuals surveyed in 27 OECD countries, 75% of respondents said that they were somewhat or very concerned about their household's finances and economic well-being. In the prior RTM survey, this figure was 8 percentage points lower, even though that edition of the survey was fielded in the middle of the COVID-19 pandemic. In 2022, almost 70% of respondents reported being worried about paying their expenses and making ends meet. The RTM survey also reveals that parents of dependent children and respondents in lower-income households were more likely to be worried about covering the costs of food, housing, energy and paying down debt.

Box 1.1. Role of the G20/OECD Task Force on Financial Consumer Protection

The OECD Consumer Finance Risk Monitor is an output of the G20/OECD Task Force on Financial Consumer Protection (the Task Force). The Task Force is the leading international forum for international financial consumer protection policy, comprising representatives of G20, OECD and Financial Stability Board (FSB) jurisdictions as well as international organisations and standard setting bodies, including CGAP, FinCoNet, IOSCO, IAIS and the World Bank. Beyond G20, OECD and FSB jurisdictions, the Task Force frequently engages with emerging markets and developing economies, including through the consultative process to review the High-Level Principles (see below), global research on the impact of COVID on financial consumers, and the development of risk dashboards (which led to the Consumer Finance Risk Monitor).

Among other things, the Task Force is responsible for the G20/OECD High-Level Principles on Financial Consumer Protection [OECD/LEGAL/0394]. In 2021-2022, the Principles in the Recommendation were reviewed and updated via a comprehensive process to incorporate policy developments that evolved over the ten years since they were first adopted (see the Infographic below for an overview of the updated Principles). This update ensured that, as the leading international standard in this area, the Principles in the Recommendation would continue to reflect global best practices and are forward-looking.

The Task Force is also responsible for the Recommendation of the Council on Consumer Protection in the field of Consumer Credit [OECD/LEGAL/0453], which was most recently updated in 2019. The Task Force will report to the OECD Council in 2024 on the implementation and continued relevance and importance of the Recommendation.

A key focus of the Task Force is the identification and consideration of issues and risks that affect financial consumers and therefore policymakers and oversight bodies responsible for financial consumer protection. The Task Force is committed to measuring and monitoring such risks via data collection and empirical analysis. To facilitate this, in March 2022 the Task Force approved a proposal to develop a periodic report on risks facing financial consumers globally, known as the Consumer Finance Risk Monitor. This is the first edition of such a report.

Infographic 1.1. G20/OECD High-Level Principles on Financial Consumer Protection

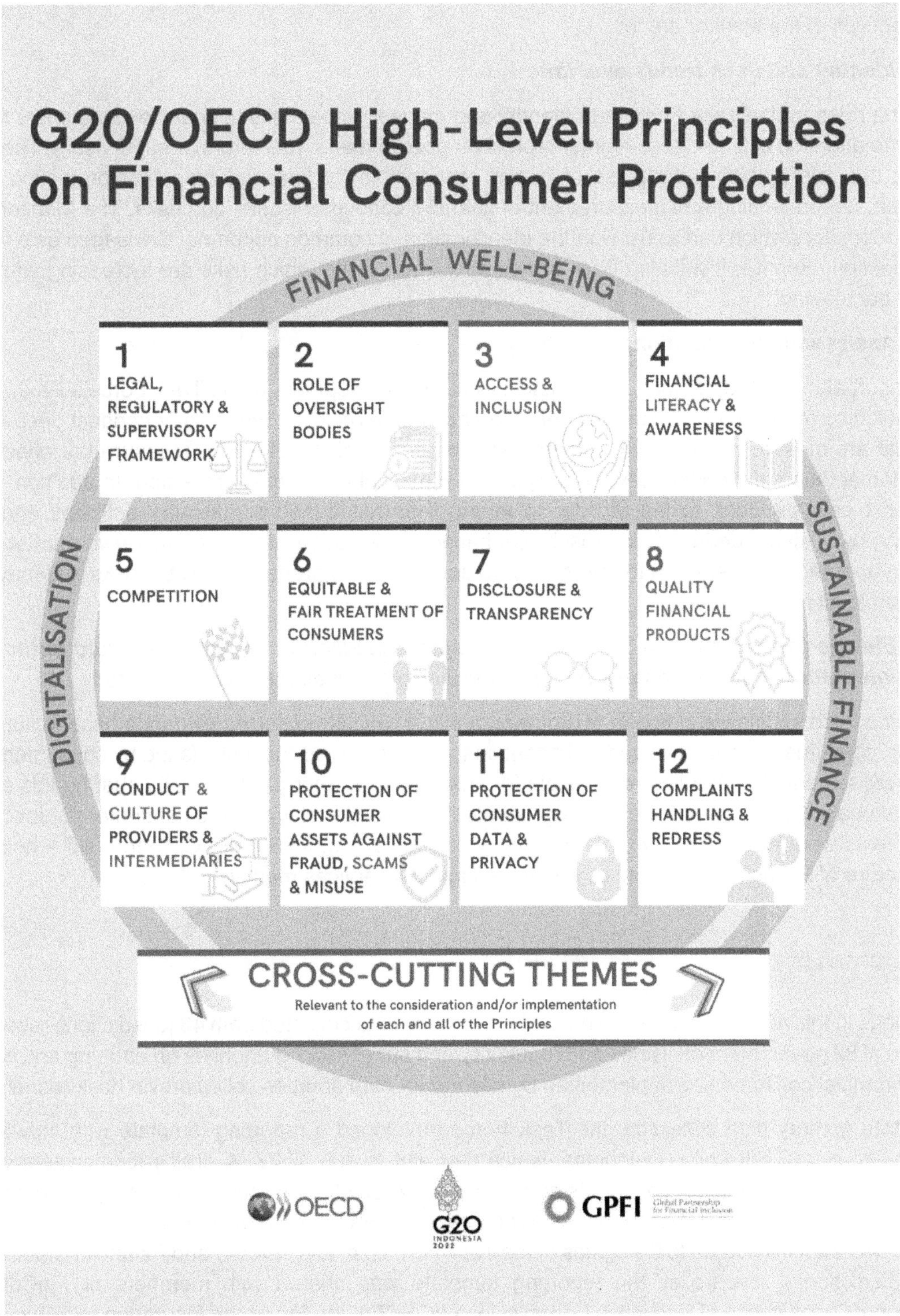

Note: Text in green colour denotes revisions made through the 2021-2022 review and update of the High-Level Principles on Financial Consumer Protection.
Source: OECD (2012[12]), "Recommendation of the Council on High-Level Principles on Financial Consumer Protection", *OECD Legal Instruments*, OECD/LEGAL/0394, OECD, Paris, https://legalinstruments.oecd.org/en/instruments/OECD-LEGAL-0394.

1.3. Objectives of the Consumer Finance Risk Monitor

The objectives of the Monitor are to:

1. ***Identify and track trends over time***

One of the roles for the Task Force is to identify and monitor global risks to financial consumers that may require the attention of financial consumer protection policymakers, regulators or supervisors. The Monitor supports this role by taking the pulse of bodies responsible for financial consumer protection on their perception, understanding and measurement of financial consumer issues and risks. The Monitor acts as a global repository which can assist with the identification of common concerns. Envisaged as a recurring data collection exercise, it will also track trends over time to see which risks are increasing, staying the same or decreasing.

2. ***Assist with prioritisation***

The Monitor, along with other inputs, can help inform the development of the Task Force's Programme of Work (including resource allocation) and help the Task Force prioritise research or conduct deep-dives on areas that are most relevant. It may also be used to help to inform efforts to measure the effectiveness and implementation of the High-Level Principles on Financial Consumer Protection. In addition, national supervisors can also look to the Monitor to inform their risk-based supervisory activities and market monitoring by mixing a deductive approach (i.e. based on risk assessments of their own markets) with a top-down approach (i.e. referring to the Monitor to anticipate and prepare for global risks that may not yet be present in all markets).

3. ***Elevate the perspective of financial consumer protection policymakers and authorities in international policy debates by contributing to the available evidence base***

The Monitor also serves the purpose of providing a systematically collected evidence base to support the "retail" or "consumer" perspective and call attention to the most important risks faced by consumers, based on the assessment of authorities responsible for financial consumer protection. By sharing this evidence in international – as well as national – policy debates, the Monitor elevates the consumer perspective and complements work carried out by other international bodies (e.g. FSB, IMF, G20) to build a holistic and global picture of the risks facing consumers in the financial services market.

1.4. Data collection and methodology

The findings in this report are based on analysis of primary data collected from 43 jurisdictions representing the views of 82 government ministries and regulatory and supervisory authorities on ongoing and emerging risks to financial consumers, complemented by secondary data sources collected via desk research.

To facilitate primary data collection, the Task Force developed a reporting template with inputs from a Working Group of Task Force Delegates, which first met in July 2022. A draft reporting template was shared with the Task Force for comments at the October 2022 Meeting. After integrating the Task Force's feedback and sharing a final draft of the reporting template with the Working Group, the finalised reporting template was then distributed to Delegates of the Task Force (i.e. G20, OECD and Financial Stability Board [FSB] jurisdictions). In parallel, the reporting template was shared with members of FinCoNet, the International Organization of Securities Commissions (IOSCO), the European Insurance and Occupational Pensions Authority (EIOPA) and the Association of Southeast Asian States (ASEAN).

The process of designing the reporting template benefitted from the Task Force's previous experience tracking consumer risks through a pilot project on Consumer Risk Dashboards and through the G20/OECD Report on Financial Consumer Protection and Financial Inclusion in the Context of COVID-19 (OECD, 2021[13]).

The reporting template collected information on three key types of risks to financial consumers. The three categories of risks to financial consumers are those stemming from the broader economic context (i.e. operating environment risks), the characteristics and circumstances of consumer themselves (i.e. demand-side risks) and the behaviour and actions of financial services providers (i.e. conduct risks). For each of the three categories, jurisdictions were asked to choose the three most significant risks to financial consumers in their jurisdiction in 2022 and indicate if they anticipated that the risk would increase, decrease, or remain the same in 2023. For each conduct risk selected, jurisdictions were further asked to identify the regulatory and supervisory actions they had taken in response.

It was important for the reporting template to also capture granular information across product sectors. Not only would this provide more detailed insights, but it would also facilitate sectoral regulators and supervisors to respond to the reporting template from the perspective of their specific market. The reporting template therefore included certain questions that split out possible responses across the following categories: banking and payments; credit; insurance; investments; and pensions. For each product market, jurisdictions were asked to identify the three products and services giving rise to the most consumer detriment in 2022 and indicate whether such detriment was expected to increase, decrease or stay the same in 2023.

Consumer detriment (see Chapter 5) was defined in the reporting template using the definition provided in the OECD Recommendation on Consumer Policy Decision Making [OECD/LEGAL/0403]. The definition is as follows:

> *the harm or loss that consumers experience, when, for example, i) they are misled by unfair market practices into making purchases of goods or services that they would not have otherwise made; ii) they pay more than what they would have, had they been better informed, iii) they suffer from unfair contract terms or iv) the goods and services that they purchase do not conform to their expectations with respect to delivery or performance.*

Separately, jurisdictions reported data on consumer complaints and financial scams and frauds.

Most of the reporting template requested data in relation to calendar year 2022 (i.e. from January to December 2022). The rationale behind this decision was that using specific beginning and end dates would facilitate easier comparisons and aggregations of data, rather than asking respondents for data from "the past year," for example. In some places, as noted above, the reporting template asked jurisdictions to describe their expectations or anticipated trends for 2023.

Data collection took place between April and August in 2023. Of the 43 jurisdictions who submitted responses, 26 of these responses represent OECD Member countries. Figure 1.6 presents a list of participating jurisdictions grouped by region. A full list of participating jurisdictions including the authorities that contributed data can be found at Annex A.

Figure 1.6. Participating jurisdictions

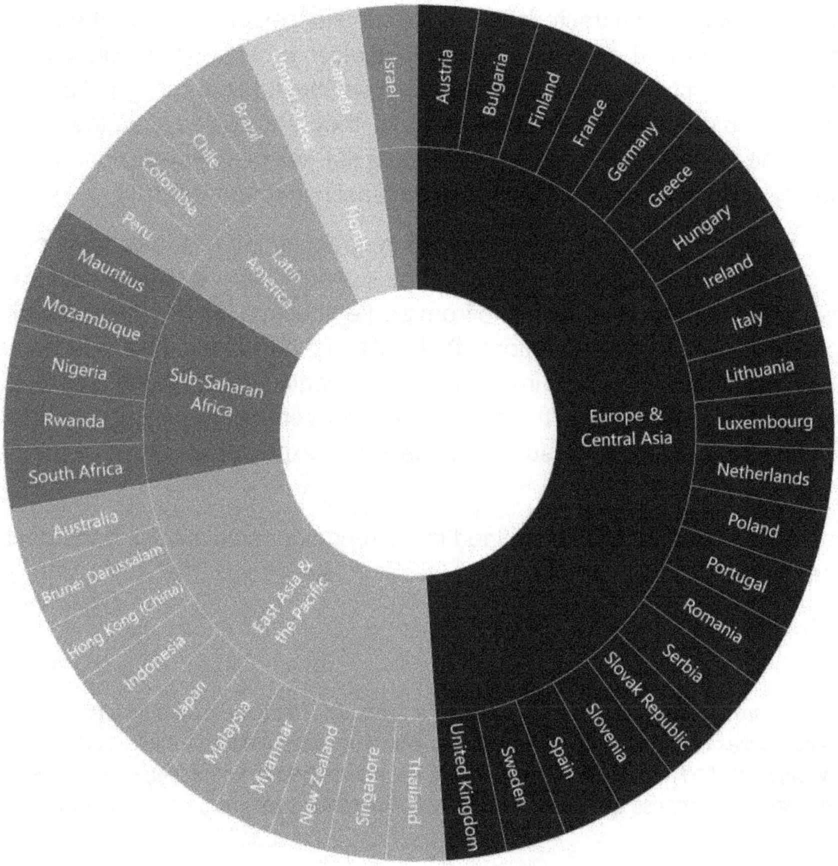

Note: Eleven G20 member countries, all seven G7 member countries, 13 of 21 APEC members and 26 OECD Member countries submitted responses to the Reporting Template.
Source: OECD Consumer Finance Risk Monitor Reporting Template 2023.

1.5. Report structure

The remainder of this report is structured in the following chapters:

- Chapter 2: Risks stemming from the operating environment
- Chapter 3: Demand-side risks
- Chapter 4: Conduct-related risks
- Chapter 5: Products and services giving rise to consumer detriment
- Chapter 6: Consumer complaints
- Chapter 7: Financial scams and frauds
- Chapter 8: Thematic risks and areas of concern, policy responses and next steps

References

Angus Reid Institute (2022), *Falling Behind: 53% of Canadians say they can't keep up with the cost of living*, https://angusreid.org/canada-cost-of-living-inflation/ (accessed on 8 September 2022). [7]

European Commission (2022), "Quarterly report on European electricity markets", Vol. 15/1, https://ec.europa.eu/info/sites/default/files/energy_climate_change_environment/quarterly_report_on_european_electricity_markets_q1_2022.pdf (accessed on 8 September 2022). [9]

Fox, M. (2022), *What's more expensive as inflation costs families extra $341 a month*, CNBC, https://www.cnbc.com/2022/05/12/whats-more-expensive-as-inflation-costs-families-extra-341-a-month-.html (accessed on 8 September 2022). [5]

International Monetary Fund (2023), *World Economic Outlook, April 2023: A Rocky Recovery*, https://www.imf.org/en/Publications/WEO/Issues/2023/04/11/world-economic-outlook-april-2023 (accessed on 14 September 2023). [4]

International Monetary Fund (2022), *G20 Background Note on Minimizing Scarring from the Pandemic*, https://www.imf.org/-/media/Files/Research/imf-and-g20/2022/g20-minimizing-scarring-from-the-pandemic.ashx. [1]

International Monetary Fund (2022), *Surging Energy Prices in Europe in the Aftermath of the War: How to Support the Vulnerable and Speed up the Transition Away from Fossil Fuels*, https://www.imf.org/en/Publications/WP/Issues/2022/07/28/Surging-Energy-Prices-in-Europe-in-the-Aftermath-of-the-War-How-to-Support-the-Vulnerable-521457 (accessed on 8 September 2022). [8]

OECD (2023), *Main Findings from the 2022 OECD Risks that Matter Survey*, OECD Publishing, Paris, https://doi.org/10.1787/70aea928-en. [11]

OECD (2023), *OECD Economic Outlook, Interim Report September 2023: Confronting Inflation and Low Growth*, OECD Publishing, Paris, https://doi.org/10.1787/1f628002-en. [3]

OECD (2023), *OECD Economic Outlook, Volume 2023 Issue 1*, OECD Publishing, Paris, https://doi.org/10.1787/ce188438-en. [2]

OECD (2021), *G20/OECD Report on Financial Consumer Protection and Financial Inclusion in the Context of COVID-19*, OECD, Paris, https://www.oecd.org/daf/fin/financial-education/g20-oecd-report-on-financial-consumer-protection-and-financial-inclusion-in-the-context-of-covid-19.htm (accessed on 8 September 2022). [13]

OECD (2012), "Recommendation of the Council on High-Level Principles on Financial Consumer Protection", *OECD Legal Instruments*, OECD/LEGAL/0394, OECD, Paris, https://legalinstruments.oecd.org/en/instruments/OECD-LEGAL-0394. [12]

Pickford, J. (2022), *UK households feel the pain of inflation*, Financial Times, https://www.ft.com/content/269bcf8d-7ee1-4050-9947-12fbb321ff03 (accessed on 8 September 2022). [6]

United Nations (2022), *Global impact of the war in Ukraine: Billions of people face the greatest cost-of-living crisis in a generation*, https://unctad.org/webflyer/global-impact-war-ukraine-billions-people-face-greatest-cost-living-crisis-generation (accessed on 8 September 2022). [10]

Note

[1] This section is adapted from an unpublished background paper prepared for the October 2022 Meeting of the G20/OECD Task Force on Financial Consumer Protection [DAF.CMF.FCP(2022)11].

2 Risks stemming from the operating environment

Certain risks that consumers face stem from the broader economic context in which they operate. This chapter reports the most significant risks stemming from the operating environment identified by responding jurisdictions. These risks include inflation and rising interest rates, financial scams and frauds, new business models and innovation along with financial market volatility.

The first category of risks to financial consumers are those stemming from the operating environment. Jurisdictions were asked to select the three most significant risks to financial consumers in their jurisdiction in 2022 and indicate if they anticipated that the significance of each of these three risks would increase, decrease, or remain the same in 2023. Figure 2.1 presents a heatmap of these risks, with the placement of each risk determined by how often jurisdictions selected it among the three most significant risks stemming from the operating environment for 2022 (the x-axis) and whether those jurisdictions expected that the significance of that risk would increase, decrease or stay the same in 2023 (the y-axis). The following key findings emerge from jurisdictions' responses to these questions:

- More than 85% of jurisdictions selected inflation and rising interest rates as one of the three most significant risks to financial consumers.
- Nearly 63% of jurisdictions selected financial scams and frauds.
- New business models and financial market volatility were slightly less represented among responses, receiving around 40% and 37% of votes, respectively. Nonetheless, as Figure 2.1 demonstrates, of the jurisdictions who chose new business models and innovation as a significant risk in 2022, relatively more of them expected that the risk would increase in 2023.
- Cyber attacks and natural disasters were selected by comparatively few jurisdictions, but these jurisdictions mostly expected that the significance of these risks would increase in 2023 (see Box 2.1 for more details on natural disasters).

Figure 2.1. Risks stemming from the operating environment

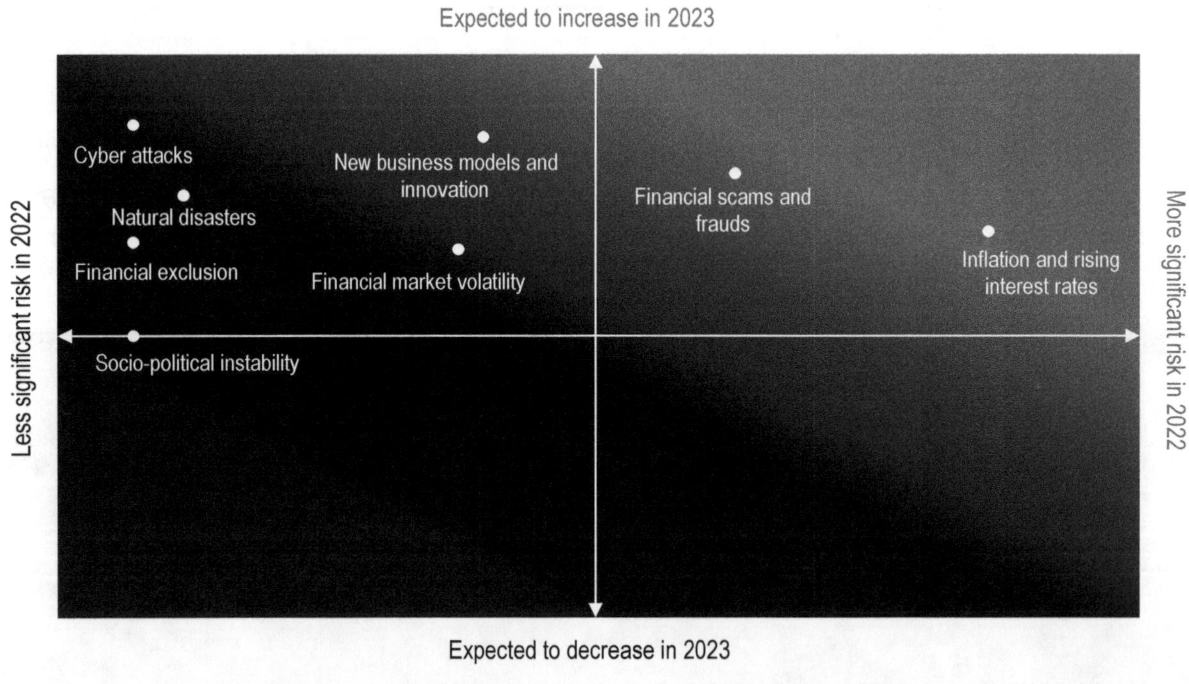

Note: The x-axis (horizontal) presents responses to questions asking for the top three operating environment risks in 2022. The y-axis (vertical) presents responses to a follow-up question asking whether jurisdictions anticipate the risk would increase, decrease, or stay the same in 2023. Risks are placed along the x-axis (horizontal) according to how frequently they were selected by respondents (more frequently selected risks are farther to the right). The intersection of the y-axis represents half the number of respondents to the question, i.e., risks to the right of the y-axis were selected by more than half of respondents. The relative positioning of the risks along the y-axis is determined by calculating an average of responses for how respondents anticipated that the risk would evolve in 2023 ("increase", "stay the same" or "decrease").
Source: OECD Consumer Finance Risk Monitor Reporting Template 2023.

2.1. Inflation and rising interest rates

The most frequently selected risk stemming from the operating environment is inflation and rising interest rates. Inflation pressures, rising costs of goods and services, and increases in interest rates all contributed to a cost-of-living crisis with a consequential impact on household finances and on households' risk of financial hardship. This is further exacerbated in jurisdictions such as **Canada**, **New Zealand** and the **United States**, which are experiencing a tightening housing market and low rental supply.

Jurisdictions noted how these broader economic trends affect the behaviours and financial well-being of consumers. For example, respondents described how inflation and rising interest rates reduced consumer savings, increased the debt-to-income ratio of borrowers, and increased the cost of borrowing, which can decrease access to credit. In **Romania**, for example, the issuance of mortgages fell by 50% in Q1 2023 compared to Q1 2022.

The impact of interest rate increases is especially notable in jurisdictions where variable-rate loans comprise a large share of outstanding home loans, which varies significantly across regions, ranging from 40% in **Luxembourg**, to 70% in **Spain** and 90% in **Poland**. In contrast, data from the Central Bank of **Ireland** showed a shift away from variable rate to fixed-rate mortgages; fixed rate mortgages accounted for 93% of the total stock of new mortgages in December 2022. Section 5.2 in Chapter 5 discusses mortgages and home loans in more detail.

Respondents also mentioned how rising interest rates led to increases in insurance premiums due to higher cost of claims and declines in pension fund contributions and—in some cases—the value of assets under management, given the loss of investment market value. **Lithuania** noted that consumers might also decide to surrender life insurance policies early to access more income to address their financial needs and meet their day-to-day expenses.

In addition to the risks outlined above, inflation and rising interest rates also increase the risk that consumers in vulnerable financial positions will be susceptible to engaging with unsuitable or even fraudulent products as a means of coping with their financial situations.

Most countries and jurisdictions anticipated that the risks driven by inflation and rising interest rates would increase or stay the same in 2023. Certain jurisdictions noted forecasts that prices would continue to increase in their markets, while others cited expectations that inflation would stabilise. In a similar vein, certain jurisdictions predicted that the majority of interest rate increases had already happened, while others warned consumers to be prepared for further rate hikes.

2.2. Financial scams and frauds

Financial scams and frauds were the second most-selected risk in the operating environment, with nearly 63% of jurisdictions ranking this risk among the three most significant. Many jurisdictions are concerned that financial scams and frauds are on the rise, given an increased use of digital finance and online payment platforms, and the search for yield and inflationary pressures that give rise to new risks. **Nigeria**, **Ireland** and **Romania** noted that such scams and frauds are becoming increasingly sophisticated. Given the increased complexity and ubiquity of financial scams and frauds, a thematic chapter is dedicated to discussing jurisdictions' experiences and approaches in dealing with financial scams and frauds; see Chapter 7 of this report for more details. Most jurisdictions noted that the incidence of financial scams and frauds increased from 2021 to 2022 and they anticipated this would continue in 2023.

2.3. New business models and innovation

Since the COVID-19 pandemic, jurisdictions have witnessed a rise in new business models and innovation. This includes an increase in the use of digital platforms, chatbots, digital assets and other fintech-related innovations. New business models and innovations witnessed in **Ontario, Canada**, for example, include private and alternative mortgage lending (including 'equity sharing' or 'rent-to-own' models), do-it-yourself (DIY) investing apps, chatbots, digital platforms, and usage-based insurance. Consumers' use of Buy Now Pay Later (BNPL) has rapidly expanded in recent years (see Box 5.1 in Chapter 5). In **Brazil**, supervisory and regulatory authorities noted a rise in banks integrating different activities and establishing partnerships with non-regulated entities.

New business models and innovation in the financial sector can help widen opportunities for financial consumers and help drive financial inclusion. The rapid pace of innovation, however, could also lead to consumer harm. For example, digitalisation has made relatively riskier products more easily accessible to consumers. New digital assets such as crypto-assets have rapidly expanded in recent years, while crypto-asset risk management and governance practices among providers lag behind (see Section 8.1.3 in Chapter 8). In **Slovenia**, for example, the lack of clarity around crypto-asset ownership rights, custody arrangements and financial representations have created a high degree of confusion for consumers. Further, hacks and outages have resulted in substantial losses for millions of consumers. Respondents were also concerned that the purported lack of a clear regulatory framework governing crypto-assets in some jurisdictions, or crypto-asset activities conducted in non-compliance with applicable domestic regulations in other jurisdictions, would increase the likelihood of fraudulent activity (see Box 5.2 in Chapter 5 for more details on regulating crypto-assets).

Digitalisation and innovation in digital products and services may also make consumers vulnerable to cybersecurity risks and scams and frauds. New business models and innovation, including the use of artificial intelligence, raise concerns regarding data protection, discrimination and bias. Most countries and jurisdictions anticipated that risks stemming from new business models and innovation would increase in 2023.

2.4. Financial market volatility

Financial market volatility was the fourth most-selected risk stemming from the operating environment. Down markets have negative effects for retail investors who are confronted with lower yields on their investments. The search for yield can also make it more likely that retail investors engage with products that do not align well with their risk profile. **Austria**, **Mauritius**, and **Spain** noted that such volatility caused uncertainty among investors. **Hong Kong (China)** and **New Zealand** noted that fluctuations in stock markets and bond prices also led to losses or reduced returns in investment funds and pension funds. In **Brunei Darussalam**, many securities offered in the country are foreign securities products, so volatility in global financial markets affects the trading prices and performance of these securities, and therefore consumers' preferences for investing in such products. Most countries and jurisdictions anticipated that financial market volatility would increase or stay the same in 2023.

Box 2.1. Natural hazards and climate change

Damages from natural hazards have grown significantly over the past 30 years, due in part to rapid economic development and climate change (OECD/The World Bank, 2019[1]). Jurisdictions reported that the impact of such hazards is dramatically affecting their citizens. **Mozambique** and **Nigeria** described how severe floods in their countries had displaced millions of people and caused large amounts of property damage. Peru noted that the Coastal El Niño phenomenon was declared in May 2023, which would bring increasing rainfall in the coastal north and drought in the South Andean region. Various regions in **Australia**, including South Australia, Victoria, Tasmania, Southeast Queensland, and New South Wales all experienced severe weather and flooding in 2021 and 2022.

Given the increased damage and losses caused by natural hazards, insurance coverage against these risks is increasingly important (OECD, 2021[2]). Natural hazards have a great impact on consumers' property and on the claims amounts that insurance undertakings must pay to policyholders. One risk to consumers (policyholders) is that insurance products that protect against disaster risks may become unaffordable as such risks become costlier to insure. When disasters occur, as articulated by **Slovenia**, it can reveal existing problems relating to the lack of clarity in the terms and conditions of insurance policies, particularly in relation to exclusions.

Australia noted a 54% increase in complaints about insurance claim delays from 2021 to 2022, which was partly attributable to disasters putting pressure on the industry.

In **Greece**, authorities are concerned that a gap in insurance protection for natural hazards could cause detriment to the financial health of consumers, especially as disasters become more commonplace. A post-disaster state relief is provided to consumers with no insurance coverage; however, the compensation is usually less than the actual amount of damage.

In **New Zealand,** climate change has impacted the affordability of (and potentially access to) financial products. Certain regions in New Zealand have recently experienced severe flooding, which has contributed to damage or loss to property (with associated financial hardship) as well as rising insurance premiums and pay-outs. The government of **New Zealand** released a severe weather exit strategy and established a task force to make recommendations for the insurability of areas impacted by severe weather events (Robertson, 2023[3]).

In 2022, the Central Bank of **Ireland** established a cross-sectoral industry forum on climate change with two working groups to address risk management and capacity building (Central Bank of Ireland, 2022[4]). These industry-led groups share examples of best practices and identify areas for further development. In March 2023, the Central Bank released guidance aiming to clarify its expectations on how (re)insurers address climate change risks in their business and to assist them in developing their governance and risk management frameworks to do this (Central Bank of Ireland, 2023[5]).

In 2022, the European Commission launched a Climate Resilience Dialogue, which explores how to address losses incurred from climate-related disasters and aims to identify how the insurance industry can contribute more to climate adaptation (European Commission, 2022[6]).

2.5. Other risks stemming from the operating environment

Relatively fewer jurisdictions selected the remaining risks stemming from the operating environment: socio-political instability, financial exclusion, operational resilience of financial institutions, cyber-attacks and limited financial infrastructure.

Regarding financial exclusion,

- Bank of **Spain** reported that new technologies could mean that people with lower digital capabilities may struggle to engage with credit institutions, especially in the context of bank branch closures.
- The **United Kingdom** noted that significant numbers of branch closures across the banking sector made it more difficult for consumers to access face-to-face services, which can often be crucial for customers in more vulnerable circumstances. The transition to digital services has led to some firms cutting back on traditional service channels, such as contact centres, in favour of online or mobile-based support solutions. Where firms are seeking to cut branches, the FCA has provided guidance to firms to help ensure they have fully considered the impact on their customer base and have established appropriate alternative solutions.
- **Sweden** highlighted a conflict between anti-money laundering regulations and the right to a payment account with basic functionality.
- The **United States** noted that gaps in fair access to financial services may encourage consumers to turn to non-banks, such as payday lenders, crypto-asset platforms and fintechs, which, while generally subject to the same consumer protection regulations, often have less stringent safety and soundness requirements and consumer oversight than banks. They may also be operating in non-compliance with applicable laws and regulations. Furthermore, notable gaps in access to basic financial services continue to exist in many low- and moderate-income communities in the United States. For example, Black and Hispanic households in the United States are around five times more likely to be unbanked than White households. The most cited reason is not having enough money to meet minimum balance requirements.

References

Central Bank of Ireland (2023), *Guidance for (Re)Insurance Undertakings on Climate Change Risk*, https://www.centralbank.ie/docs/default-source/regulation/industry-market-sectors/insurance-reinsurance/solvency-ii/requirements-and-guidance/guidance-re-insurance-undertakings-on-climate-change-risk.pdf?sfvrsn=a232991d_6 (accessed on 19 September 2023). [5]

Central Bank of Ireland (2022), *Central Bank of Ireland hosts inaugural meeting of the Climate Forum and publishes Sustainable Investment Charter*, https://www.centralbank.ie/news-media/press-releases/central-bank-of-ireland-hosts-inaugural-meeting-of-the-climate-forum-and-publishes-sustainable-investment-charter-30-june-2022 (accessed on 19 September 2023). [4]

European Commission (2022), *Climate Resilience Dialogue*, https://climate.ec.europa.eu/eu-action/adaptation-climate-change/climate-resilience-dialogue_en (accessed on 19 September 2023). [6]

OECD (2021), *Enhancing Financial Protection Against Catastrophe Risks: The Role of Catastrophe Risk Insurance Programmes*, OECD, Paris, http://www.oecd.org/daf/fin/insurance/Enhancing-financial-protection-against-. [2]

OECD/The World Bank (2019), *Fiscal Resilience to Natural Disasters: Lessons from Country Experiences*, OECD Publishing, Paris, https://doi.org/10.1787/27a4198a-en. [1]

Robertson, G. (2023), *Cyclone Taskforce to ensure locally-led recovery*, https://www.beehive.govt.nz/release/cyclone-taskforce-ensure-locally-led-recovery (accessed on 19 September 2023). [3]

3 Demand-side risks

Demand-side risks relate to the characteristics and circumstances of consumers themselves. This chapter reports the most significant demand-side risks identified by responding jurisdictions. These risks include lack of financial literacy, over-indebtedness, lack of digital capability and insufficient income. The chapter also discusses additional sources of financial consumer vulnerability.

The second category of risks relates to the characteristics and circumstances of consumers. Figure 3.1 presents a heatmap of these demand-side risks, with the placement of each risk determined by how often jurisdictions selected it among the three most significant demand-side risks for 2022 (the x-axis) and whether those jurisdictions expected that the significance of that risk would increase, decrease or stay the same in 2023 (the y-axis). The following key findings emerge from jurisdictions' responses to this question:

- Some 73% of jurisdictions selected lack of financial literacy as one of the three most significant demand-side risks in 2022.
- Over-indebtedness was selected by more than half of jurisdictions, and lack of digital capability was selected by around 43%.
- Every demand-side risk was expected to increase in significance in 2023 with the exception of lack of financial literacy.

Figure 3.1. Demand-side risks

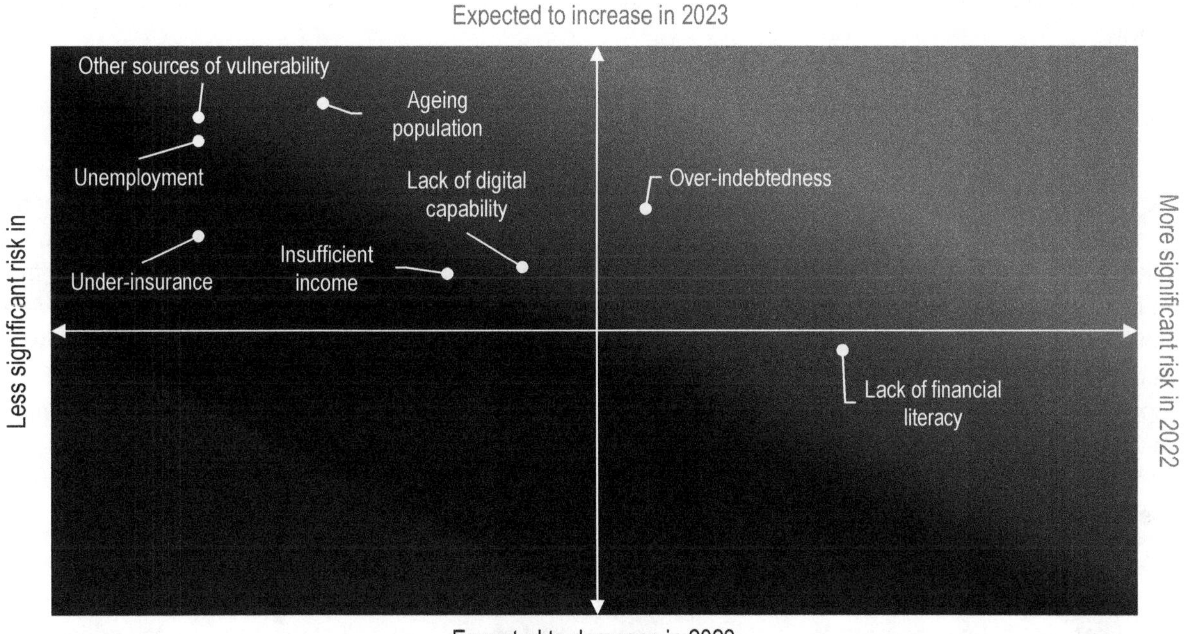

Note: The x-axis (horizontal) presents responses to questions asking for the top three demand-side risks in 2022. The y-axis (vertical) presents responses to a follow-up question asking whether jurisdictions anticipate the risk would increase, decrease, or stay the same in 2023. Risks to the right of the y-axis were selected by more than half of respondents.
Source: OECD Consumer Finance Risk Monitor Reporting Template 2023.

3.1. Lack of financial literacy

The most selected demand-side risk is the lack of financial literacy. Given the macroeconomic environment, many consumers are facing financial challenges. For consumers with low levels of financial literacy, financial management can be confusing and stressful because the marketplace for financial products and services is complex and changing at a rapid pace. Jurisdictions noted that given the complexity of the financial landscape, many consumers may lack an adequate understanding of the risks and opportunities of the financial products and services they use. In **Indonesia**, for instance, improvements in financial literacy are lagging behind growing levels of financial inclusion, suggesting a lack of awareness and understanding among consumers regarding the financial products and services they use. **Greece** and **Slovenia** mentioned that part of this lack of understanding stems from the fact that many consumers find the terms and conditions to be written in language that is too technical, or that the descriptions of financial products and services are full of jargon with which the average consumer is unfamiliar. Beyond financial literacy, this observation highlights how financial firms may fail to implement effective disclosures (see Section 4.2 in Chapter 2). **Peru** also noted that low levels of financial literacy may be associated with a lack of trust in formal financial institutions, further impairing these consumers' abilities to manage their daily finances. Low levels of financial literacy also pose a risk to consumers if they are unable or unwilling to actively engage in financial planning such as planning for retirement (**Singapore**).

Jurisdictions mentioned financial education initiatives to help address low levels of financial literacy, (see Section 8.2.4 in Chapter 8). Other jurisdictions including **Israel** and **New Zealand** noted the relative shortage of campaigns to promote financial literacy, despite its relevance and importance. As consumers face more sophisticated and complex financial instruments, this may also put them at risk of misuse or being victims of financial scams and frauds.

On average, jurisdictions anticipated that significance of this risk would slightly decrease in 2023. In general, jurisdictions noted that despite improvements in recent years, gaps in financial literacy persist. Even as consumers gain skills and knowledge, they noted, the complexity of products on offer continues to grow.

3.2. Over-indebtedness

The second most-selected demand side risk is over-indebtedness. Considering the macroeconomic situation with elevated interest rates and high inflation, jurisdictions are concerned that consumers could make greater use of credit to meet financial obligations, which would increase indebtedness. Results from the Financial Consumer Agency of **Canada**'s COVID-19 Financial Well-being Survey showed that overall debt levels of Canadians had increased since 2019. The survey results also showed that Canadians were becoming more likely to borrow to pay for daily expenses, while the rise of consumers with insufficient income to meet daily expenses also led to an increase in reverse mortgages, private mortgages and more individuals being under-insured. The **United Kingdom** noted that many debt advice charities and consumer organisations had reported an increase in demand for debt advice, especially from those in the most desperate circumstances.

Jurisdictions noted that this trend of over-indebtedness is exacerbated by the rise of new products and services such as Buy Now Pay Later and payday lending. **South Africa** and **Thailand** noted the high costs for households to be over-indebted; some households must spend over half of their income to service debt. **Slovak Republic** emphasised how over-indebtedness could also threaten the stability of the financial sector. On average, jurisdictions anticipated that over-indebtedness would increase in 2023, citing a range of factors including rising interest rates, wage increases lagging behind inflation, rising unemployment and increased uptake of alternative and in some cases unregulated means of obtaining credit (e.g. Buy Now Pay Later, payday loans, illegal money lending). See Box 5.1 in Chapter 1 for details on BNPL and Section 4.1.1. in Chapter 4 for details on responsible lending regulation.

3.3. Lack of digital capability

The third most-selected demand side risk is a lack of digital capability. The quick growth of new business models, the digitalisation of the financial sector and the rapid growth of fintech innovation make digital capabilities even more vital. However, consumers with lower levels of digital literacy or limited digital capabilities may be excluded from increasingly digitalised processes. As noted in responses from a number of jurisdictions, consumers who lack digital capabilities could face reduced access to banking services, especially if bank branches close. **Hungary** noted that consumers who lack reliable internet access and smartphones cannot access information that is provided on websites or social networking sites. **Mauritius** noted that a growing elderly population calls attention to levels of “tech-savviness” among elderly consumers. Jurisdictions agreed that consumers with low levels of digital capability and digital financial literacy would find it difficult to engage with the financial sector and could be more susceptible to harm, including financial scams and frauds. This could include, for instance, situations where consumers are not able to make fully informed decisions and fall prey to pushy sales techniques such as pre-ticked boxes to purchase insurance for a product. Countries and jurisdictions anticipated that the significance of this risk would increase in 2023, in part due to demographic trends.

3.4. Insufficient income

Insufficient income was selected by nearly 40% of jurisdictions as one of the most significant demand-side risks in 2022. This risk is closely tied to over-indebtedness and rising interest rates and inflation. Many jurisdictions were concerned about how households could support themselves on inadequate incomes when the costs of living and borrowing were increasing significantly. In **Peru**, the pandemic significantly affected the financial resilience of Peruvians as around 85% of the population, at some point, were not able to cover their expenses with their income. This situation caused Peru’s poverty levels to rise to 27.5% in 2022 (which meant a setback to levels last seen in 2011).

Further, respondents highlighted how insufficient income could force consumers to make financial decisions that could further heighten their vulnerability (e.g. taking payday loans, forfeiting insurance policies). On average, jurisdictions expected that the significance of this risk would increase in 2023, due to wages not increasing sufficiently to keep pace with general costs of living.

3.5. Other sources of vulnerability

Relatively fewer jurisdictions selected the remaining demand-side risks: ageing population, underinsurance, unemployment and other sources of vulnerability.

- *Ageing population.* Respondents from **Canada**, **Greece**, **Italy**, **Japan**, **Mauritius, Poland, Romania** and **Singapore** expressed concern over their ageing populations and the impact this would have on their economies, social safety nets and financial well-being of society. Jurisdictions foresaw that financial vulnerability of retail investors could increase, due to lower digital competences of the elderly. Moreover, as people live longer and the workforce shrinks, individuals will face an uphill struggle to fund longer retirements.
    - Since 2018, the ACPR (Prudential Supervision and Resolution Authority) and the Autorité des marchés financiers of **France** have conducted work on marketing of financial products to vulnerable elderly populations. The aim of this work is to make all stakeholders safer and to limit the risk of mis-selling for these customers and financial institutions. Based on initial work in 2020 the authorities called on professionals in the insurance, banking and financial sector to exercise enhanced due diligence on vulnerable older customers and to apply by 2022 the findings of thematic workshops held in 2020.
- *Consumers experiencing vulnerability.* Beyond specific demographic groups, such as the elderly, jurisdictions also mentioned increasing numbers of consumers generally experiencing financial vulnerability as a significant demand-side risk. In the **United Kingdom**, for example, a May 2022 survey found that over half of all UK adults showed one or more characteristics of vulnerability. In general, vulnerability could stem from different factors, including natural catastrophes, temporary income shocks, or consumers with health issues or a disability. This also could include consumers who have limited fluency and/or literacy in the official language of their jurisdiction. Jurisdictions that selected this demand-side risk anticipate that this risk will increase in 2023.

Box 3.1. Consumer vulnerability and the G20/OECD Task Force on Financial Consumer Protection

Consumer vulnerability and related topics such as financial well-being are strategic themes for the Task Force especially in light of factors such as the experience of the COVID-19 pandemic and changing economic conditions. The updated High-Level Principles on Financial Consumer Protection also underscore the importance of paying special attention to the treatment of consumers who may be experiencing vulnerability. In this context, the Task Force approved a workstream on "Understanding and Responding to Consumer Vulnerability" in October 2022. This workstream aims to:

- articulate an understanding of consumer vulnerability and how it is relevant in the context of financial services
- analyse policies relating to consumer vulnerability in the context of financial consumer protection
- identify effective approaches to this subject.

The output of the project will be a report by the Task Force on the development, implementation and effectiveness of protections for consumers experiencing vulnerability, including identifying effective approaches and examples from jurisdictions. The aim of the report will be to assist jurisdictions that are developing or enhancing their approach to consumer vulnerability and support the implementation of the High-Level Principles on Financial Consumer Protection.

4 Conduct-related risks

Conduct-related risks arise from the behaviour and actions of financial services providers. These risks include poor-value financial products and services, ineffective disclosures, poor financial advice, dishonest sales practices and unsuitable product design. In addition to describing the most significant risks to financial consumers stemming from the conduct of financial institutions, this chapter also highlights the regulatory and supervisory actions taken to address these risks in 2022 and presents information on the tools used to monitor conduct risks in the financial sector.

The third broad category of risks comprises those that arise from the conduct of financial institutions. Figure 4.1 presents a heatmap of conduct-related risks, with the placement of each risk determined by how often jurisdictions selected it among the top three conduct risks for 2022 (the x-axis) and whether those jurisdictions expected that the significance of that risk would increase, decrease or stay the same in 2023 (the y-axis). The following key findings emerge from jurisdictions' responses to this question:

- Half of responding jurisdictions selected poor-value financial products and services and lack of or ineffective disclosures as significant risks in 2022.
- Poor financial advice and unsuitable product design were selected by one third of jurisdictions, and dishonest sales practices and unauthorised financial activities were selected by around 30%.
- Respondents anticipated that the significance of these conduct risks, with a few exceptions, would remain the same in 2023.
- While the misuse of data as a conduct risk was only selected by three jurisdictions, the outlook for it in 2023 in those jurisdictions is much more pessimistic compared to the other conduct risks.

Figure 4.1. Conduct risks

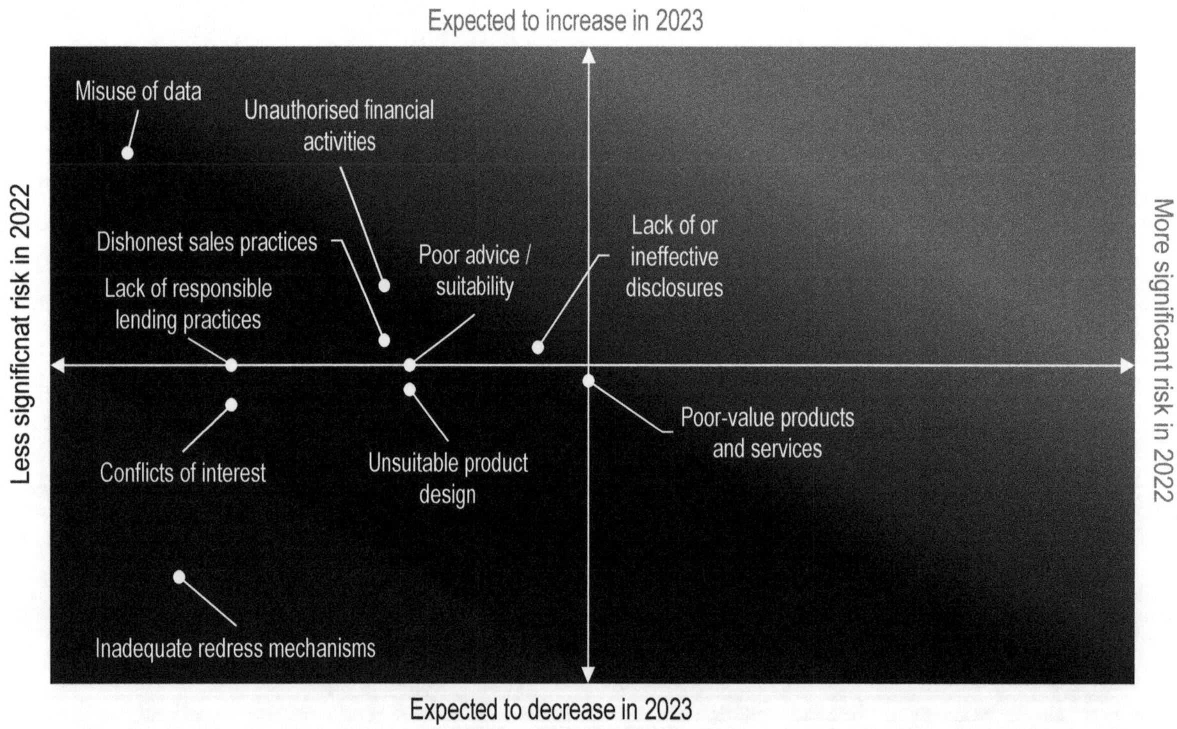

Note: The x-axis (horizontal) presents responses to questions asking for the top three conduct risks in 2022. The y-axis (vertical) presents responses to a follow-up question asking whether jurisdictions anticipated that the risk would increase, decrease, or stay the same in 2023. The placement of the y-axis corresponds to half the number of respondents (i.e. poor-value products and services was selected by exactly half of responding jurisdictions; the other risks were selected by less than half).
Source: OECD Consumer Finance Risk Monitor Reporting Template 2023.

Policymakers and regulatory and supervisory bodies can undertake a range of actions to address risks to financial consumers, thereby strengthening overall levels of financial consumer protection. This chapter describes the top five conduct risks selected by jurisdictions and the regulatory and supervisory actions taken to mitigate these risks.

4.1. Poor-value financial products and services

The most significant conduct risk chosen by jurisdictions was products and services with poor value. While financial scams and frauds (as referenced in Chapters 2 and 7) may lead to a sudden loss in assets, the cumulative loss of wealth caused by poor-value products and services can have a significant material impact on household budgets and contribute to a loss of trust in financial institutions and the financial system.

In contrast to poor value products and services, the G20/OECD High-Level Principles on Financial Consumer Protection [OECD/LEGAL/0394] describe quality financial products in the following passage:

> *Quality financial products are those that are designed to meet the interests and objectives of the target consumers and to contribute to their financial well-being. There should be appropriate product oversight and governance by financial services providers, and where appropriate, by intermediaries, to ensure that quality financial products are designed and distributed.*

Whether a product or service delivers value for money or can be qualified as "quality" depends on a range of factors, which can include overall costs, pricing structures, added value for consumers, complexity, the proportion of costs that go to commissions or distribution fees and comparison of costs with those of competitors. In the context of insurance products, claims ratios (i.e. the percentage of total collected premiums which is paid back to consumers through claims) can help to assess value for money. For investment products, expected rates of return (in comparison to the costs charged and investment strategy pursued) and profitability for issuers may be considered. As noted in a report from the European Securities and Markets Authority, value-for-money is determined based on "investor utility, including the costs of purchasing a product, the expected or realised benefits, as well as other factors such as product quality" (European Securities and Markets Authority, 2023[1]).

The macroeconomic conditions of 2022 may have created additional pressure on financial service providers' profit margins, which could negatively affect consumers if they are advised to purchase products and services that do not provide adequate value. Jurisdictions noted that poor value financial products may also be a result of not enough competition in the investment or pension markets. **Germany**, **Indonesia, Lithuania** and **Slovenia** referenced unit-linked insurance and other insurance-based investments as examples of potentially poor value products.[1] The Financial Conduct Authority of the **United Kingdom** noted that the pace and scale at which firms pass through higher base interest rates to savers were slow and low, and needed to improve. **Peru** and **the United States** also mentioned that excessive fees, sometimes referred to as "junk fees," continued to be a problem in their respective jurisdictions.

4.1.1. Regulatory and supervisory actions

Figure 4.2 shows the most common regulatory and supervisory actions taken by countries and jurisdictions in response to poor-value financial products and services. The most common action was discussions with industry participants, followed by sending supervisory letters and issuing guidelines or supervisory statements.

Figure 4.2. Regulatory and supervisory actions taken in 2022 to address poor value financial products and services

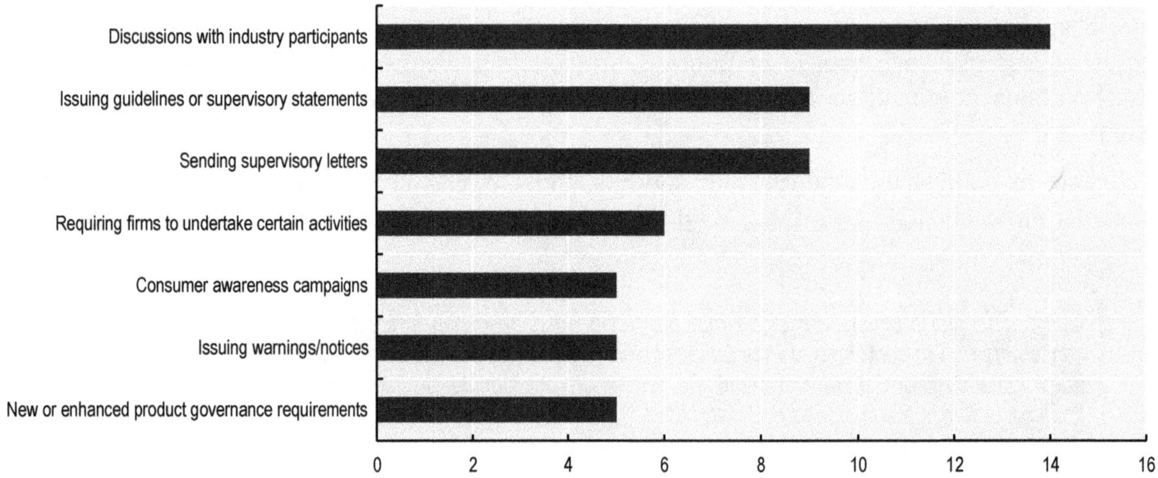

Note: N=21.
Source: OECD Consumer Finance Risk Monitor Reporting Template 2023.

Several jurisdictions increased their oversight and monitoring of the imposition of fees and charges, in some cases leading to additional guidance, regulation or enforcement actions. **Israel** expanded the supervision of fees linked to current accounts to freeze current prices levels for certain services (Bank of Israel, 2022[2]), and Banco de **Portugal** performed inspections in 2022 to assess compliance with the prohibition of charging fees for the renegotiation of loan conditions, among other requirements for lenders. The Portuguese Securities Market Commission also focused on the theme of value for money in 2022 (Comissão do Mercado de Valores Mobiliários, 2023[3]), developing and applying a new methodology to supervise the value for money of structured notes, and supporting the development of a forthcoming methodology to be applied to investment funds. The Ontario Securities Commission (**Canada**) addressed excessive fees cases related to investments in a series of nine settlements, the most recent of which resolved in 2022. In general, the cases related to charging clients higher fees even when their account holdings rose beyond a threshold that entitled them to a lower fee rate or double-charging client fees (i.e. putting clients in proprietary funds which charged fees, while also charging management fees on the client assets).

To gather data on fair value metrics, **South Africa** introduced enhanced reporting indicators. The indicators are currently limited to the insurance sector, with plans to roll out this type of reporting to help assess fair value across financial institutions. A thematic review was also conducted on premium increases in the life insurance sector, and a further review is planned around fees and disclosures for banking products. In another example from the insurance sector, the European Insurance and Occupational Pensions Authority (EIOPA) carried out an extensive analysis of the unit-linked and hybrid insurance-based investment products market which resulted in a Supervisory Statement and the development of a common methodology on how to assess value for money. The Statement and methodology provide further guidance on how product governance requirements should be implemented to ensure value for money. **New Zealand** similarly issued value-for-money guidance in the managed investment scheme sector to support industry participants to better understand how to deliver good value financial products and services. In **France**, the ACPR and the AMF have been working together on increasing transparency and cost containment. In 2022, the ACPR launched a dialog with representatives of the insurance industry and public authorities (AMF and Treasury) on diagnostic elements relating to administrative arrangements designed to moderate the fees and charges of unit-linked life insurance policies.

Bank of **Thailand** issued regulations in 2022 setting out six guiding principles on practices and disclosures regarding interest, charges and penalties for financial products and services (Bank of Thailand, 2022[4]). Among other things, the principles dictate that the collection of interest, service charges, and penalties from customers must be appropriate, and prices and rates must be fair, not exploitative, and not redundant. In determining prices and rates, the service providers must consider the actual costs incurred from the business operations. In addition, service providers must not put excessive burdens on customers and must consider their ability to pay.

Jurisdictions have also introduced regulation or legislation to ban certain practices related to fees and charges: **Ireland** banned price-walking[2] in home and motor insurance, while **Romania** made legislative changes that eliminated one of the two types of fees charged by private pension funds. The Consumer Financial Protection Bureau of the **United States** issued advisory opinions and guidance statements explaining how junk fees can be illegal.

While value for money risks can arise in the context of different financial products, jurisdictions are particularly concerned about excessive costs in the credit market:

- Under the **Australian** Securities and Investments Commission's (ASIC) product intervention powers, ASIC made product intervention orders in relation to short-term credit and continuing credit contracts where ASIC saw significant consumer detriment, prohibiting the issue of these loans. ASIC also took action in relation to predatory lending, high-cost credit and misconduct impacting borrowers experiencing financial difficulty.
- **Brazil** enacted a new law in 2021 aiming to prevent and mitigate over-indebtedness. The law establishes a "minimum existential value" (i.e. the minimum amount a person should have in order to pay their basic expenses to live) and other responsible lending practices, including advertisement standards.
- **Finland** reported plans to lower the interest rate ceiling for consumer loans.
- Bank of **Israel** published guidelines on consumer credit management, which included directives related to the marketing of point-of-sale credit and guidelines related to housing loans to enhance transparency, comparability and the simplification of customer agreements.
- The Bank of **Italy** issued guidelines on revolving credit with the aim to address market conduct issues it had previously detected resulting in poor-value financial products and services.
- **Peru** introduced a cap on interest rates for new personal loans, personal loans of small amounts and new loans to small and micro-sized firms. Peru also introduced regulation to enhance product governance regarding interest rate monitoring for compliance with usury laws. Additionally, late fees on past-due loans were banned, and limitations were placed on the retroactive application of interest on the principal portion of past-due loan instalments or payments.

Box 4.1. Low-fee accounts: a tool to promote value for money

A range of jurisdictions have implemented programmes or policies in recent years aiming at expanding access to basic financial services that deliver value for money. Beyond expanding financial inclusion, these programmes may also support value for money by identifying key features that should be made available to all consumers.

In **Australia**, ASIC reviewed banks' compliance with an obligation to provide low or no-fee accounts to low-income consumers. The review found that some individuals in high-fee transaction accounts, including First Nations people, were paying up to 3000 AUD in overdraw fees over a year. The review revealed that banks were aware of high numbers of customers eligible for low-fee accounts but that the majority of banks' processes to transfer these eligible customers to low-fee accounts were ineffective.

ASIC wrote to the banks outlining their key findings and expectations going forward (Australia Securities & Investments Commission, 2023[5]).

In the **European Union**, Directive 2014/92/EU established the right to a basic payment account for all consumers legally residing in the European Union (including consumers with no fixed address, asylum seekers and consumers who have been refused a residence permit but whose expulsion is impossible for legal or factual reasons). (Some European countries, including Portugal, have had similar programmes in place since before the introduction of the Payment Accounts Directive in 2014.) The Directive also strengthened the requirements for banks to disclose their fees, which helps customers to compare offerings and made it easier for customers to switch banks. The Directive further requires that banks provide payment accounts with basic features "free of charge or for a reasonable fee". According to an assessment published in 2023, some European countries have transposed this into their legislation by requiring that the accounts be provided for free, while others have implemented fee limits (European Commission, 2023[6]).

In **India**, the Pradhan Mantri Jan-Dhan Yojana (PMJDY) programme was launched in 2014 to expand access to financial services in the country. Through the programme, individuals can open a Basic Savings Bank Deposit Account (BSBDA) (Reserve Bank of India, 2014[7]). The BSBDA has no minimum balance requirements and earns interest. The package also includes a debit card, accident insurance and an overdraft facility.

After **Peru**'s introduction of basic savings accounts in 2011 as a tool for financial inclusion, in 2018 the Superintendency of Banking, Insurance and Private Pension Funds (SBS) passed regulation (SBS Resolution N° 2891-2018) to enhance their definition and market conduct regulation. These accounts are subject to transaction and balance limits but can be opened by both nationals and foreign residents under a simplified KYC regime. The regulation includes disclosure requirements prior to contracting these basic accounts, including costs, obligations and channels for users to raise complaints or report loss of credentials. Additionally, within the framework of the National Financial Inclusion Policy, the Government approved the Law 31120 (2021), which allowed the National Bank of Peru (Banco de la Nación) to open a digital ID account ("Cuenta DNI") for all citizens over 18-years-old. This product is a digital basic savings account that aims to promote citizens' financial inclusion, simplifying social transfers and other financial operations. By 2022, 13.1 million ID accounts were created, representing 58% of Peruvian adults.

The National Bank of **Serbia** issued a by-law in August 2022 regarding payment services needed for everyday activities (National Bank of Serbia, 2022[8]). The by-law defines the guaranteed features of a "payment account" package and limits the prescribed price of the package. Citizens who choose this package can open a dinar current account in a bank, withdraw cash at the tellers and ATMs of their bank free-of-charge, receive a free-of-charge debit card and benefit from mobile and e-banking with an unlimited number of transactions at POS via QR codes. There is also the possibility to upgrade this package with additional services such as an FX account, credit card, overdraft or cheques, without the need to switch to a more expensive package.

In the **United Kingdom**, the nine largest providers of current accounts have been legally required since 2015 to offer basic bank accounts to customers who do not have an account or who are ineligible for the bank's standard account. The basic bank accounts do not include overdraft facilities, and there are no fees for standard operations. In all other respects, they must provide the same services as a standard account. As of June 2022, more than 7 million basic bank accounts were open at the nine institutions (HM Treasury, 2023[9]).

4.2. Lack of or ineffective disclosures

The second most significant conduct risk selected by jurisdictions was ineffective disclosures. It is important that financial information is presented to consumers in language that is clear and not misleading. Jurisdictions noted that terms and conditions are often not properly disclosed to clients at the pre-contractual stage, the time of purchase, or during the life of the product. The lack of or ineffective disclosures may be detrimental to consumers if the consumers do not properly understand the cost and potential risks of the products and services they are purchasing. **Ireland** and **Italy** noted that this risk is heightened in the case of products and services that are not regulated and/or distributed by non-professional intermediaries, such as linked credit agreements distributed by dealers of goods and services and in the case of products such as Buy Now Pay Later. **Canada** and **Luxembourg** noted that enhanced disclosure requirements are a key focus of their financial consumer protection regulatory frameworks and supervisory actions. Jurisdictions anticipated that the impact of the lack of or ineffective disclosures would remain the same in 2023.

4.2.1. Regulatory and supervisory actions

As articulated in the G20/OECD High-Level Principles on Financial Consumer Protection, financial services providers and intermediaries should provide consumers with key information on a product's fundamental benefits, risks and terms. Providers should communicate this information in an effective and clear manner so that consumers can make informed decisions about which products and services best fit their needs. Yet many jurisdictions noted that terms and conditions are often improperly disclosed to clients at the pre-contractual stage, at the time of purchase, or during the life of the product. As shown in Figure 4.3, the most common action taken in response to this risk was sending supervisory letters, followed by new or enhanced disclosure requirements and discussions with industry participants.

Figure 4.3. Regulatory and supervisory actions taken in 2022 to address the lack of or ineffective disclosures

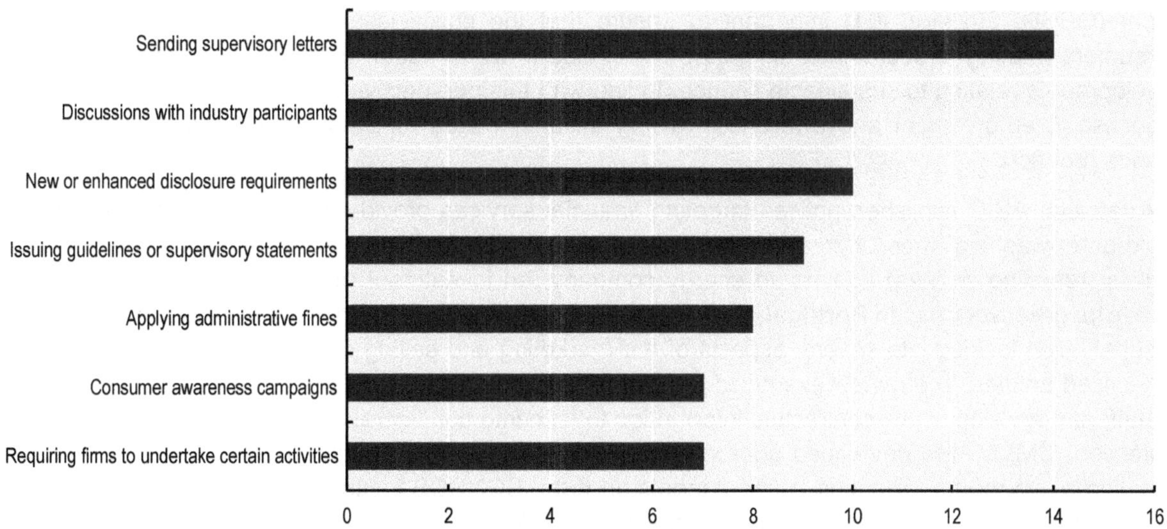

Note: N=19.
Source: OECD Consumer Finance Risk Monitor Reporting Template 2023.

In an example of sending supervisory letters, Bank of **Spain** sent letters to inform institutions of possible breaches of regulations relating to the provision of information to consumers, examples of which included payment accounts, switching of accounts and mortgages. Bank of **Israel** also published supervisory letters and regulatory directives on the issue of disclosure to customers, for example on fees and notices sent to customers. The authority also published specific guidelines and directives on disclosures in payment applications and credit marketing.

Regarding new or enhanced disclosure requirements, the new Financial Consumer Protection Framework in **Canada** went into effect in June 2022 and introduced new disclosure obligations for banks, such as providing key information at important milestones in the product cycle (i.e. renewals, promo offer ending, interest rate changing). **Spain** also introduced new or enhanced disclosure requirements in 2022 for certain pre-contractual and in-contract information obligations regarding revolving credit products. **Peru** enacted regulation to improve reporting requirements concerning the fees and charges that financial institutions may impose on customers and established standardised denominations and categories that financial institutions can use when disclosing such fees and charges to clients.

Several jurisdictions described carrying out supervisory activities aimed at overseeing the implementation of disclosure requirements. The Financial Consumer Agency of **Canada**, for example, launched a thematic review with 12 banks in 2022 to evaluate how they have implemented new electronic alert obligations, as well as assessing their effectiveness. Securities supervisors in Europe participated in European Securities and Market Authority's (ESMA) 2022 Common Supervisory Action and mystery shopping exercise regarding compliance with disclosure requirements for costs and charges under the Markets in Financial Instruments Directive (MIFID) II. The Financial Market Authority of **Austria**, for example, discussed the results of this exercise with the industry and issued administrative fines in cases of infringements. In **Italy**, CONSOB (the securities regulator) focused on assessing how firms complied with Key Information Document requirements related to packaged retail investments and insurance products (PRIIPs), while Bank of Italy developed a desk-based analysis of the websites of several banks and financial intermediaries to verify the clarity of the information provided to the public.

A key theme related to disclosure that has emerged recently concerns environmental social and governance (ESG) and sustainable finance. As articulated in a 2023 OECD Business and Finance Policy Paper (OECD, 2023[10]), it is important to ensure that the policy issues, opportunities and risks for consumers relating to sustainable finance are included in the broader international policy and markets developments relating to sustainable finance. In line with this perspective, several jurisdictions described supervisory, enforcement and awareness-raising actions related to ESG disclosures and sustainable finance products.

In **Australia**, ASIC published notices targeting financial services providers, including one titled "How to avoid greenwashing when offering or promoting sustainability-products". ASIC also issued infringement notices (resulting in fines) against an energy company, an investment manager and a superannuation trustee for greenwashing. In **Portugal**, CMVM (the securities regulator) carried out in 2022 the first exercise of supervision looking into several aspects of the marketing and selling of ESG financial instruments by supervised entities. The review examined firms' business practices, investors' ESG preferences, training of staff, and revision of pre-contractual information to take into consideration ESG regulation and investor protection. CMVM also developed publications and content on sustainable finance aimed at investors, including a two-month campaign in social media. In **Italy**, CONSOB focused supervisory activity on ESG disclosures provided by asset management companies (AMCs). For new AMCs authorisations, CONSOB focusses on how sustainability issues are integrated into the investment process in relation to the type of investment funds that the company intends to manage. CONSOB also maps the sustainability policies published on AMCs' websites, evaluates ESG disclosure practices in relation consistency between the reported ESG characteristics and the investment process, and analyses marketing communications concerning investment funds offered to the public that are characterised by ESG profiles.

4.3. Poor financial advice and failure to perform suitability assessments

Poor financial advice and the failure to perform suitability assessments was the third-most selected conduct risk. Some jurisdictions considered that, given the broader macroeconomic climate, consumers may look to reduce costs and could purchase financial products and services that are cost-effective yet not adequately suited to their needs. Consumers might also be advised to buy products and services that they do not fully understand, and which may not be properly suitable for them. Some jurisdictions are worried that consumers are getting poor advice from non-professionals such as young influencers through social media (see Section 8.1.5 in Chapter 8 for more details). Other jurisdictions point to companies and institutions themselves failing to provide appropriate products to consumers (who may lack enough knowledge to recognise that the product or service they are purchasing is not appropriate for their needs). **Japan** and **Mozambique** both noted the importance for financial institutions to have a consumer-oriented business conduct as they develop and market their products and services. **Canada** specifically mentioned a plan to crack down on predatory lending to vulnerable people by lowering the Criminal Rate of Interest within the Canadian Criminal Code and capping charges by payday lenders.

4.3.1. Regulatory and supervisory actions

Figure 4.4 shows regulatory and supervisory actions most frequently taken by jurisdictions in response to poor advice and failure to perform suitability assessments. Sending supervisory letters comprised the top response, followed by consumer awareness campaigns.

Figure 4.4. Regulatory and supervisory actions taken in 2022 to address poor advice and failure to perform suitability assessments

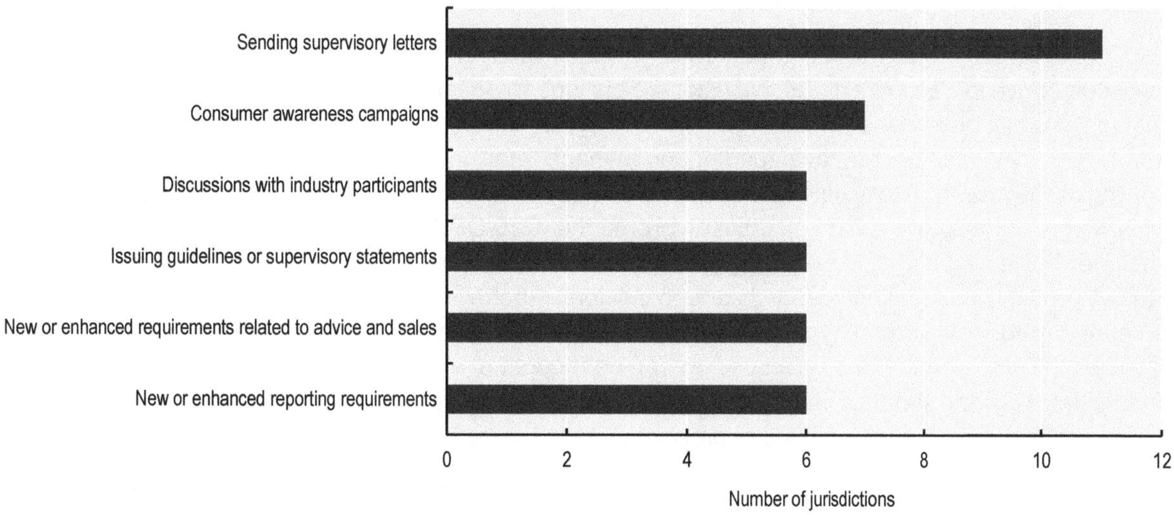

Note: N=14.
Source: OECD Consumer Finance Risk Monitor Reporting Template 2023.

The Superintendencia Financiera de **Colombia** (SFC), for example, sent supervisory letters demanding that firms providing financial advice meet all requirements mentioned in the applicable law regarding advisory services. In addition, SFC shared best practices with entities to enhance information disclosure mechanisms and specialised advisory process. The Central Bank of **Hungary** (MNB) conducted a thematic review revealing non-compliance with requirements for assessing suitability; MNB followed up with investment firms to improve their suitability assessment procedures, in line with the findings from the review. In **Bulgaria**, some investment firms were similarly given recommendations to improve the questionnaires provided to investors when performing suitability assessments.

In **Ireland**, a review of some complex investment products (known as Structured Retail Products, or SRPs) found poor practices and weaknesses in firms which increased risks to investors. In response, the Central Bank of Ireland required firms to identify a sufficiently granular target market for SRPs and to drive improvements in the quality and transparency of disclosures to investors of the risks relating to these products.

In **Hong Kong (China)** the Insurance Authority (IA) issued codes and guidelines addressing conduct risks arising from poor advice and the failure to assess suitability of products. Moreover, IA issues periodical publications (i.e. Conduct in Focus) to examine topical regulatory issues and set out its expectations on how the insurance industry should conduct business. At the end of 2022, IA's edition of Conduct in Focus took a "name and shame" approach in order to remind insurers, insurance broker companies and insurance agencies to get the basics right in their controls over their agents and technical representatives with respect to compliance of the Continuing Professional Development required hours.

The Banco de **Portugal** assesses compliance with the provision of advice and suitability requirements via inspections, including mystery shopping, targeting retail products including mortgages, consumer credit and deposit accounts. These assessments also address compliance with assistance duties applicable to the commercialisation of those products through digital channels, which presents specific challenges. The main irregularities detected are related to poor advice, irrespective of the commercialisation channel, the lack of or misleading information about product characteristics in the pre-contractual/contractual phase and pre-selected product options.

4.4. Unsuitable product design

While unsuitable product design is related to the risk of poor value financial products and services, addressed above in Section 4.1, the two risks are distinct. Unsuitable product design results from a lack of adequate product governance within firms. Product governance can be defined as "The procedures and controls in place to design, approve, market and manage retail financial products through their life cycle to ensure that they meet, at any time, the interests and objectives of consumers and the relevant regulatory requirements" (FinCoNet, 2021[11]). As set out in the G20/OECD High-Level Principles on Financial Consumer Protection [OECD/LEGAL/0394] such requirements may include defining a target market for a financial product, conducting research and considering behavioural insights to understand the target market and, depending on the type, complexity and risk of the product, carry out testing before launching the product. Thus, unsuitable product design can be thought of as one channel through which poor value financial products and services come to market. At the same time, products and services may fail to deliver value simply because their costs are not proportionate to the benefits accrued by consumers.

In **Luxembourg**, the insurance supervisory authority, Commissariat aux Assurances, found only a few insurance undertakings testing insurance products with respect to customers' interests either before introducing these products to the market or before modifying them. In **Romania**, an analysis of the terms and conditions of home insurance products revealed that many conditions relating to insured risks applied to all customers, irrespective of the type of property (house/apartment) and the area in which it is located. This resulted in a mismatch between the insured risks with the actual needs of the customers in the target market. Unsuitable product design poses a risk to financial consumers if the products and services available in the marketplace do not support consumers' financial well-being.

4.4.1. Regulatory and supervisory actions

Figure 4.5 shows the regulatory and supervisory actions most frequently taken by countries and jurisdictions in response to unsuitable product design, the most common of which were discussions with industry participants and sending supervisory letters.

Figure 4.5. Regulatory and supervisory actions taken in 2022 to address unsuitable product design

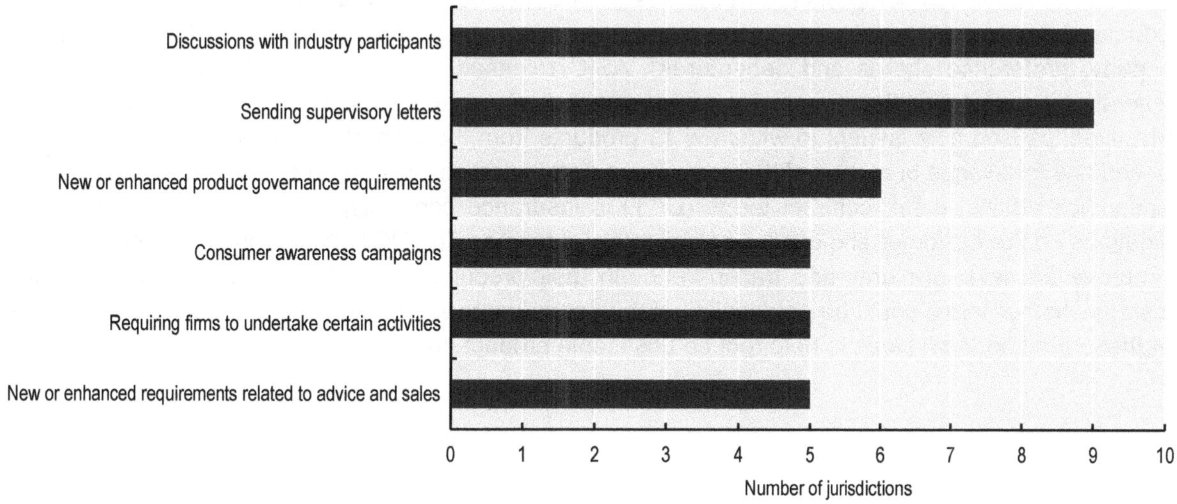

Note: N=13.
Source: OECD Consumer Finance Risk Monitor Reporting Template 2023.

Bank **Indonesia** noted that consumers believe that many financial products offered in their jurisdiction are not suitable for their business or needs. This risk may also result from a lack of product detail or information. In response to these concerns, Bank Indonesia conducted discussions with industry to strengthen their product descriptions and educate consumers on the characteristics of various products.

In **Poland**, where 90% of mortgages are variable rate, the Office of Competition and Consumer Protection reported that while the redesign of the mortgage market is a complex issue, steps have been taken to introduce more long-term fixed-rate lending and standardised contracts, given that such products would be more suitable and beneficial to financial consumers.

In **South Africa**, the Financial Sector Conduct Authority is strengthening supervisory engagements with institutions to assess product design and governance processes to determine if gaps exist in the existing regulatory framework and standards. Currently, product design and governance requirements are split between one set of rules for insurance products and another for banking products. In the future, the regulator intends to introduce overarching and harmonised conduct legislation that would specifically address product design and governance issues across financial products and institutions.

The National Securities Market Commission of **Spain** (CNMV) reported carrying out several supervisory actions in response to data reported periodically by firms providing investment services to verify that firms had acted in the interest of the client when designing and/or distributing financial instruments. CNMV sent supervisory letters to firms requiring the adoption of corrective measures when needed. In 2022, Spain also modified an existing law regarding credit institutions, introducing a new obligation for credit institutions to develop policies and procedures, including appropriate internal control mechanisms, in relation to product governance and oversight. The modification aims to ensure that banking products and services are designed taking into account the needs, characteristics and objectives of the target market for which they are intended and are marketed through appropriate channels.

Regarding the insurance sector, **Italy** reported supervisory actions aimed at verifying the implementation of product oversight and governance (POG) processes for insurance-based investment products, with a particular focus on assessing value for money of the products in relation to the identified target market and the methodologies used in the post-sale monitoring. As a result of these inquiries, Italy reported that insurers were improving POG processes and revising their value for money assessment models. In some cases, insurers revised features of the examined product or even stopped selling products that had failed to meet cost and performance expectations.

In 2022, ASIC reviewed compliance with the design and distribution obligations by issuers of investment products in **Australia** (i.e. interests in managed investment schemes, shares issued by an investment company, preference shares and debentures). ASIC released a report in 2023 summarising its key observations, noting significant room for improvement. It also issued a stop order relating to credit and derivatives, caused nine issuers to withdraw 11 products from the market, and commenced civil penalty proceedings for alleged breaches of the design and distribution obligations. In parallel, ASIC commenced proceedings against unfair contract terms (UCT) in insurance contracts, where terms impose unclear obligations on the customer and can lead to negative outcomes The UCT protections encourage insurers to improve the level of clarity and transparency in their products, as well as encouraging insurers to consider whether terms could be potentially unfair to consumers when design their products. ASIC notes that these are important steps to help reduce unsuitable product design.

4.5. Other conduct risks

4.5.1. Dishonest sales practices

The fifth most significant conduct risk selected by jurisdictions was dishonest sales practices (tied with unauthorised financial activities). Dishonest sales practices may include unfair charges or unfair computation of charges, mis-selling and misleading advertisements. Dishonest sales practices can arise in a range of contexts, from unauthorised firms misrepresenting themselves to employees of licensed firms acting unethically and untruthfully. For example, when firms make bonuses or employment contracts contingent upon unrealistic sales targets, this can purposely or inadvertently encourage dishonest or illegal practices. Mis-selling in ESG or sustainable finance includes the risk that firms are not adequately or correctly integrating sustainability principles or misrepresenting the degree of sustainability through a process known as greenwashing, which may lead to inadequate investment decisions regarding sustainable finance. Dishonest sales practices can also be found in aggressive marketing techniques or in the use of "dark patterns", particularly in light of digitalisation trends. Dark patterns, which were referenced by **Lithuania**, **Slovenia** and **Spain**, refer to a range of methods commonly deployed in digital user interfaces that lead them to make choices that may not be in their best interests, often through exploiting consumer biases (OECD, 2022[12]).

Two of the most frequent regulatory and supervisory actions taken by countries and jurisdictions in response to dishonest sales practice include issuing warnings/notices and consumer awareness campaigns. Regarding warnings, notices and supervisory letters, the National Securities Market Commission (CNMV) of **Spain** carried out several supervisory actions to detect aggressive marketing practices regarding complex and risky financial instruments, resulting in supervisory letters sent to firms requiring corrective measures. In some cases, the CNMV published warnings on its website. The Financial Markets Authority of **New Zealand** reported a deliberate increase in action against issuers of wholesale offers (i.e. not available to retail investors) who had produced dishonest or misleading disclosures. The Financial Services Commission of **Mauritius** suspended licenses and in other cases referred matters to its Enforcement and Settlement Committees for applicable administrative sanctions.

To address the issue of dishonest sales practices in mandatory provident fund schemes (pensions) in **Hong Kong (China)** the Mandatory Provident Fund Schemes Authority (MPFA) gave guidance to the industry in the form of circulars and held discussions with industry participants. Depending on the nature and seriousness of misconduct cases, appropriate disciplinary actions were taken by the MPFA, such as suspension of or disqualification from registering as an intermediary. To better understand the selling practices of intermediaries with respect to two tax-deductible products, the MPFA collaborated with the Hong Kong Monetary Authority and the Insurance Authority to conduct their first-ever joint Mystery Shopping Programme on the selling practices of these products. The authorities issued a joint circular with key findings and good practices (Hong Kong Monetary Authority, Insurance Authority and Mandatory Provident Fund Schemes Authority, 2022[13]).

Examples of consumer awareness campaigns can be found in **Bulgaria**, the **European Union**, **Japan** and **Malaysia**:

- The Financial Supervision Commission of Bulgaria conducts initiatives and programmes to help consumers develop knowledge, skills and confidence to make informed financial decisions. Regarding dishonest conduct, the Commission also issues warnings to enhance consumer awareness. Bulgaria further noted that Key Information Documents conveying consumer rights can prevent consumers from being misled.
- Regarding dark patterns, EIOPA carried out reviews in selected Member States and uncovered a series of dark patterns. As a result, EIOPA published online guidance for consumers (EIOPA, n.d.[14]) and shared information with relevant national competent authorities.
- Japan's Financial Services Agency monitors the activities of financial institutions to determine if they align with the "Principles for Customer-Oriented Business Conduct" (Financial Services Agency, 2017[15]). By formulating the Principles and publishing a list of financial institutions that have adopted the Principles and developed and published their own policies, the JFSA encourages financial consumers to choose financial services providers that are more likely to act honourably in their sales practices.
- In Malaysia, regulators focussed on educating consumers about insurance products and provided guidance in choosing the right insurance policy that suits their needs and budget. Policy developments also centred on enhancement on disclosure and sales practices requirements for informed decision making when purchasing insurance products, as well as strengthening the roles and responsibilities of the board and senior management.

4.5.2. Unauthorised financial activities

Thirteen jurisdictions ranked unauthorised financial activities among the three most significant conduct risks in 2022. In **New Zealand**, authorities witnessed a rise in the number of unregistered financial products and providers, particularly in FX margin trading. In **South Africa**, unregulated financial institutions try to entice customers with promises of "super" returns on investments; the Financial Sector Conduct Authority (FSCA) is actively trying to educate and encourage South Africans to verify the registration of financial institutions with the FSCA before engaging in any financial activities. In **Italy**, the most common type of unauthorised activity reported to CONSOB (the securities regulator) relates to contract-for-differences involving crypto-assets. In **Luxembourg**, the Commission de Surveillance du Secteur Financier (CSSF) has received increasing number of complaints from consumers regarding suspicious or unauthorised service providers attempting to offer their services. Often, these providers are fraudsters pretending to be a supervised entity in order to steal money from victims. Fraudulent platforms are usually well-designed to trick consumers into believing they are credible.

In **Chile**, the Financial Markets Commission (CMF) is responsible for authorising a range of prudentially regulated financial institutions that may offer credit in the market. However, there is currently no general legal framework requiring entities offering credit to consumers to be authorised or registered before being permitted to undertake consumer credit activities. This gap limits the authorities' abilities to supervise financial consumer protection issues. While the national consumer authority (SERNAC) can take action *ex post* based on wrongdoing by such entities, in a context of high interest rates and decreasing access to consumer credit from entities under CMF supervision, respondents from Chile noted that they expected the participation of unauthorised financial activities to increase in the market.

4.5.3. Additional conduct risks

Other conduct risks include lack of responsible lending, conflicts of interest, inadequate redress mechanisms and misuse of data and algorithms.

- *Lack of responsible lending.* Seven jurisdictions ranked the lack of responsible lending practices among the top three conduct risks in their jurisdictions. Authorities are concerned about new credit products, such as Buy Now Pay Later, as products of smaller amounts and shorter durations that could lead to a relaxation of responsible lending practices. In some jurisdictions, like **Australia** for example, responsible lending practices have largely protected consumers from incurring unaffordable debt in the context of more mainstream products (such as mortgages and credit cards), while concerns have been raised about their lack of effectiveness in the context of payday loans/consumer leases and their absence in the context of Buy Now Pay Later products. The **United States** noted that the most significant financial consumer risk was irresponsible lending practices adopted by some members of industry. This may manifest itself in many ways, such as junk fees charged to consumers or through a lack of proper oversight by lenders over new products proliferating in the marketplace (including Buy Now Pay Later). Bank of **Spain** sent letters of recommendations to inform institutions of possible breaches of responsible lending regulations. Bank of **Thailand** issued new regulation on responsible lending, effective as of 2024, which aims to alleviate household over-indebtedness by ensuring that lenders treat consumers responsibly and fairly throughout the debt journey, including through setting out measures for persistently indebted borrowers (Bank of Thailand, 2023[16]).
- *Conflicts of interest.* Conflicts of interest may occur given certain business practices and business models, particularly with commission-based sales as mentioned by responses from **Italy**, **Germany**, **Lithuania**, **Slovenia** and **Thailand**. In **Lithuania**, for example, insurance agents are the main unit-linked insurance sales channel, and they receive a large commission for the sale of such products. The Bank of Lithuania's mystery shopping exercise on unit-linked insurance sales in 2022 revealed shortcomings in determining customer needs, assessing product suitability and disclosing pre-contractual information, all issues which may be exacerbated given the commission-based sales structure in place for these types of insurance products. Conflicts of interest can also arise in the joint sale of credit protection insurance with mortgages.
- *Inadequate redress mechanisms.* As set out in the G20/OECD High-Level Principles on Financial Consumer Protection, complaints handling and redress mechanisms must be "accessible, affordable, independent, fair, accountable, timely and efficient". Five jurisdictions selected inadequate redress mechanisms as one of the top 3 conduct-related risks in 2022. Regulators and supervisors in **Poland**, for example, are concerned with how the redress mechanism for unauthorised financial transactions (as codified in the Payment Services Directive [PSD] 2) is functioning in the banking sector.
- *Misuse of data.* One potential misuse of data is if customers' data is offered to third parties and then used to market and sell additional products and services without the customers' consent. A second potential misuse of data, which is a focus of the CFPB in the **United States**, is the increased use of algorithmic models in financial decision making by lenders and the potential for bias in these models that may weaken access to credit to historically disadvantaged communities and communities of colour.

4.6. Regulatory and supervisory tools used to monitor conduct risks

In addition to asking jurisdictions to rank the top conduct risks, the reporting template also collected information on the tools that regulators and supervisory authorities used to monitor conduct risks in the financial sector. As shown in Figure 4.6, the most frequently used tools to monitor risk include complaints data, assessing reporting information from regulated and/or supervised institutions, engaging with industry stakeholders, conducting surveys of financial institutions and/or thematic reviews and participating in international organisations and convenings. Mystery shopping, advanced data analytics, surveys of consumers, regulatory sandboxes and social media monitoring are less common regulatory and supervisory tools used to monitor risks to financial consumers.

Figure 4.6. Tools used to monitor conduct risks

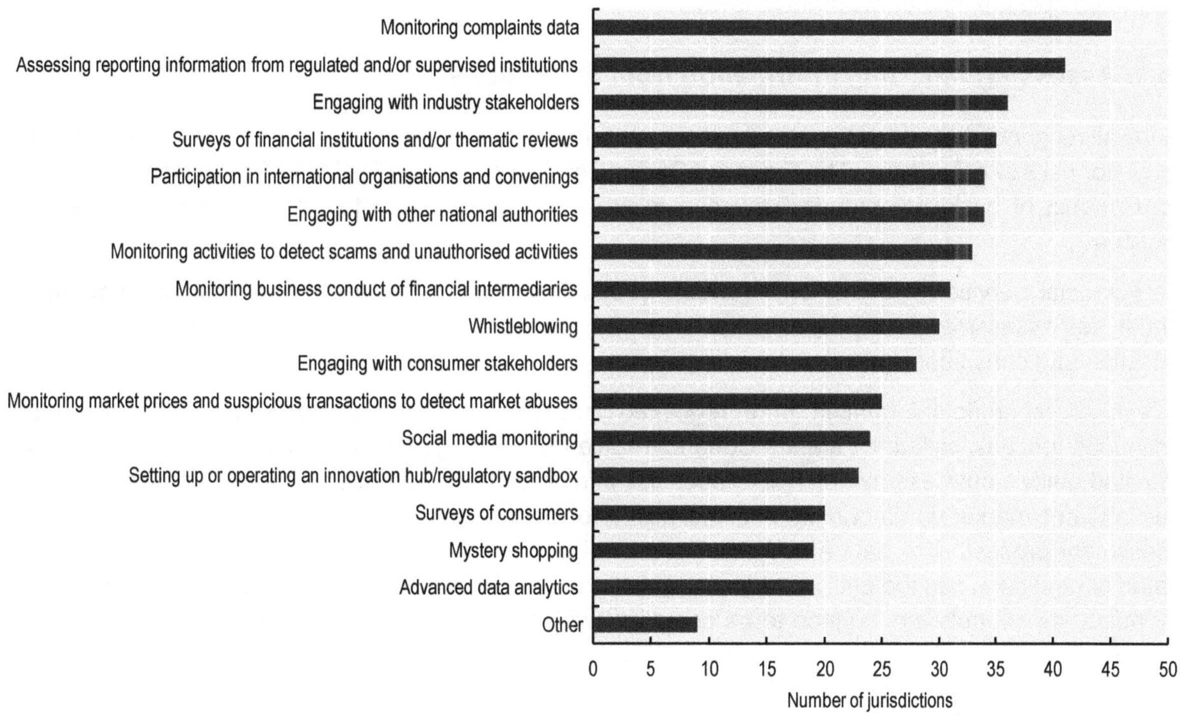

Note: N=46.
Source: OECD Consumer Finance Risk Monitor Reporting Template 2023.

4.6.1. Monitoring complaints data

Monitoring complaints data is the most common regulatory and supervisory tool used to monitor risks to financial consumers, selected by 100% of respondents. In **Canada**, the Financial Consumer Agency of Canada (FCAC) monitors complaints directly from consumers via a consumer call centre. Furthermore, a new Financial Consumer Protection Framework adopted in 2022 legislatively obligates banks to report individual information on complaints received, including detailed information on the nature of the complaint, on a quarterly basis to the FCAC. The first set of these reports was provided to the FCAC in November of 2022. A Reporting, Analytics and Data Team is tasked with the analysis of this reported information. In **Serbia,** financial institutions must provide detailed complaints data including the total number of complaints, the type of complaint, and the number of complaints granted in favour of consumers. This data may trigger on-site supervision if the number of complaints is not proportionate to the size of the bank and/or the number of consumers. At the end of 2022, SBS **Peru** introduced an updated regulatory framework for handling complaints, which included the obligation for financial institutions to provide comprehensive monthly reports on complaints and to provide SBS direct access to their complaint databases.

Often, complaints data was used by authorities to inform further regulatory and supervisory work such as on-site supervision and serve as a basis for quarterly or annual risk assessment exercises. Regulators and supervisors in **Rwanda** and **Colombia** found that monitoring complaints via Twitter was particularly helpful.

Certain jurisdictions use complaints data to inform their own risk dashboards and indicators. For instance, in **Hong Kong (China)** the Hong Kong Monetary Authority monitors complaints data and publishes a "Complaints Watch" to highlight the latest complaints trends in the banking sector and emerging topical issues. In **Romania**, the Financial Supervisory Authority developed a Conduct Risk Indicators dashboard at both the market and firm level. This dashboard automates the indicators calculation process. In addition, ASF developed a Tableau Risk Indicators on Complaints which, among other things, allows the ASF to analyse complaints data at the product level.

4.6.2. Assessing reporting information from institutions

Nearly all responding jurisdictions reported using information collected from regulated institutions as a way to monitor risks to consumers. The Financial Sector Conduct Authority (FSCA) of **South Africa** noted that the "Conduct of business" reports they receive are a key off-site monitoring tool for their supervisory functions.

The Financial Services Authority of **Indonesia** (OJK) OJK requires supervised institutions to submit an annual self-assessment report on compliance with consumer protection regulations through OJK's education and consumer protection reporting system.

To assess reporting information from regulated institutions, FCAC (**Canada**) uses a defined and continuous process, called the Market Conduct Profile (MCP), to gather and analyse information about a regulated entity's business model. FCAC uses this information to differentiate regulated entities based on their inherent market conduct risks and the ability to manage those risks. The main intent of the risk assessment process is to gain a deeper understanding of the adequacy of the entity's market conduct related controls (i.e. can the entity demonstrate that it understands applicable market conduct obligations, that adequate controls are in place to be compliant with MCOs, and that it effectively deals with issues when they arise).

4.6.3. Industry and consumer engagement

Collaboration with other entities – including industry stakeholders, consumer stakeholders and other authorities – emerged as a common tool. The National Bank of **Rwanda**, for example, described holding meetings with the representatives on consumer protection regulations and launching a forum with other stakeholders including consumers' associations, other consumer protection regulatory authorities and the ombudsman office.

Central Bank of **Ireland** reported significant engagement with stakeholders including consumer representative bodies, civil society groups and industry representatives, holding 13 structured stakeholder engagements with key stakeholders between April and October 2022.

In **Hong Kong (China)**, the Hong Kong Monetary Authority maintains close contact and collaboration with the Consumer Council of Hong Kong, primarily in the areas of policy engagement (i.e. seeking feedback and support from the Consumer Council when devising major banking consumer protection policies) and incident handling (i.e. working with the Consumer Council upon emergence of major consumer protection incidents, such as credit card scams), to gain intelligence regarding relevant consumer concerns in order to comprehensively assess and thus handle the consumer protection incidents.

Regarding surveys of consumers, **FCAC** (Canada) described regularly conducting public opinion research surveys to assess various consumer experiences and impressions, including experiences of hardship. For example, in November 2022, FCAC published findings on consumer vulnerability from its monthly COVID-19 Financial Well-being Survey (Financial Consumer Agency of Canada, 2022[17]).

4.6.4. Co-ordinating with international and domestic counterparts

International co-operation was another common strategy for regulators and supervisory bodies to monitor risks to financial consumers. **Canada, Hong Kong (China), Italy, Japan, Portugal** and **Spain** mentioned engagement with the OECD and FinCoNet, the International Financial Consumer Protection Organisation. Many regulators and supervisors also noted engagement with other national and local authorities to monitor risks to financial consumers and address consumer detriment. In **Hong Kong (China)** the HKMA participates in the Fraud and Money Laundering Intelligence Taskforce which helped retail banks identify over 19 000 previously unknown mule accounts. The HKMA also collaborates with the Consumer Council of Hong Kong when devising major banking consumer protection policies and handling consumer protection incidents.

4.6.5. Advanced data analytics

Relatively fewer jurisdictions use advanced data analytics in their regulatory and supervisory work. The Austrian Financial Market Authority (**Austria**) is looking at using machine learning to better analyse complaints data. At the Institute for the Supervision of Insurance (IVASS) in **Italy,** a new IT application for complaints management publishes a "white list" with sites and domains of authorised intermediaries in the insurance sector to help combat the spread of ghost broking (i.e. when a fraudster poses as a representative of an insurance company to sell a fake insurance policy). IVASS also worked with an external vendor to use AI algorithms to evaluate the simplicity and clarity of insurance contracts. Regulators at the CONSOB in **Italy** use advanced data analytics in co-operation with an Italian university to develop AI methods to detect suspicious trading activity. After having previously launched a pilot, **Peru** implemented in 2022 a social media monitoring tool to conduct sentiment analysis of social media posts and comments by users. The tool covers the four largest banks and the four largest credit card providers, thus providing SBS with weekly and monthly reports on the topics most commented and the institutions involved.

Advanced data analytics is also used to help monitor reporting information. In **Spain,** advanced data analytics are used to analyse reporting information on market conduct since a new circular from Banco de España came into force in 2022. Regulators and supervisors in **Ireland** evaluate social media monitoring data provided by an external vendor.

4.7. Effectiveness of monitoring tools

According to respondents, the most effective tools used to monitor risks to financial consumers is the ability of regulatory and supervisory bodies to monitor market prices and suspicious transactions to detect market abuses and surveys of financial institutions. National Bank of **Rwanda** reported monitoring market prices for certain services (e.g. deposit fees, account closing fees, early repayment charges) and prohibiting fees that seemed unfair to consumers.

As shown in Figure 4.7, surveys of financial institutions and/or thematic reviews, monitoring business conduct of financial intermediaries, monitoring complaints data and advanced data analytics are also seen as very effective tools that regulatory and supervisory bodies use to monitor risks in their jurisdictions. Social media monitoring, regulatory sandboxes and whistleblowing were considered less effective tools to monitor risks to financial consumers.

Figure 4.7. Effectiveness of tools used to monitor conduct risks

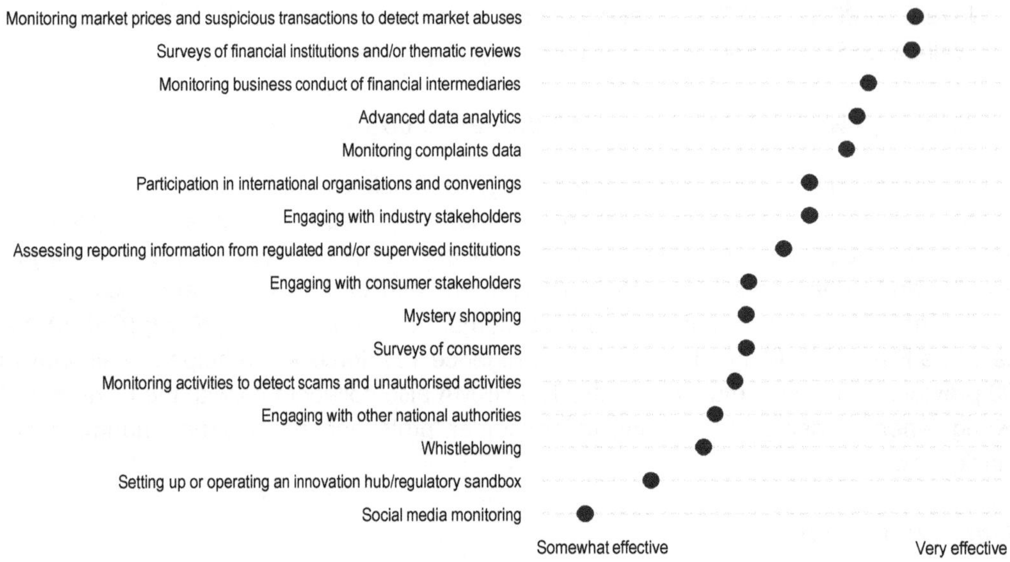

Note: N=46. The relative "score" of each regulatory or supervisory tool is determined by calculating an average of responses for the effectiveness of the corresponding tool ("very effective", "somewhat effective" or "not effective").
Source: OECD Consumer Finance Risk Monitor Reporting Template 2023.

4.8. Plans to amend or add new tools

In addition to the regulatory and supervisory tools discussed above, some jurisdictions are planning to add new regulatory or supervisory tools in the upcoming year.

- *Mystery shopping.* **Hungary**, **Israel**, **Italy**, **Romania**, **Rwanda** and **Serbia** added or planned to add (or expand) their use of mystery shopping as a supervisory tool. Additionally, a legislative proposal in **Spain** would include mystery shopping as a new supervisory tool of Banco de España.
- *Advanced data analytics.* **Austria**, **Canada**, **Germany**, **Indonesia**, **Ireland**, **Italy**, **Portugal** and the **United Kingdom** mentioned expanding their use of advanced data analytics to support their regulatory work. Bank **Indonesia** intends to create a consumer protection indicator or index using advanced data analytics to better monitor issues of consumer protection in their jurisdiction. In 2022, Banco de **Portugal** implemented a new SupTech tool to automate the validation of draft credit agreement, which institutions are legally required to report to the Banco de Portugal. It is currently developing a new SupTech tool for monitoring advertisements for retail banking products and services.
- *Social media monitoring.* **Ireland**, **Luxembourg**, **Nigeria**, **Peru** and **Thailand** plan to increase their use of social media monitoring given the increased use of social media and the potential for consumers to access misleading information.
- *Whistleblowing.* Authorities in **Israel** are writing a supervisory procedure on whistleblowing. Authorities in the **Netherlands** are looking into ways to reward whistle-blowers.

References

Australia Securities & Investments Commission (2023), *ASIC acts to ensure better banking outcomes for Indigenous consumers*, https://asic.gov.au/about-asic/news-centre/find-a-media-release/2023-releases/23-183mr-asic-acts-to-ensure-better-banking-outcomes-for-indigenous-consumers/ (accessed on 25 August 2023). [5]

Bank of Israel (2022), *The Banking Supervision Department is expanding supervision of current account fees*, https://www.boi.org.il/en/communication-and-publications/press-releases/the-banking-supervision-department-is-expanding-supervision-of-current-account-fees/ (accessed on 19 September 2023). [2]

Bank of Thailand (2023), *BOT announces new measures to sustainably address household debt problems*, https://www.bot.or.th/en/news-and-media/news/news-20230721.html (accessed on 19 September 2023). [16]

Bank of Thailand (2022), *Notification of the Bank of Thailand No. SG2. 7/2565*, https://www.bot.or.th/content/dam/bot/fipcs/documents/FPG/2565/EngPDF/25650048.pdf. [4]

Comissão do Mercado de Valores Mobiliários (2023), *CMVM publishes annual circular notes for issuers, financial intermediaries, and asset managers*, https://www.cmvm.pt/PInstitucional/Content?Input=9D949DF75A4ED8339639483D370EC7C5C4A49C38E35F775433761DD51AAA6C65 (accessed on 19 September 2023). [3]

EIOPA (2023), *Supervisory statement on differential pricing practices in non-life insurance lines of business*, https://www.unepfi.org/wordpress/wp-content/uploads/2021/05/PRB-Guidance-Financial-Inclusion.pdf (accessed on 19 September 2023). [18]

EIOPA (n.d.), *Dark patterns in insurance: practices that exploit consumer biases*, https://www.eiopa.europa.eu/tools-and-data/behavioural-insights-insurance-and-pensions-supervision/dark-patterns-insurance-practices-exploit-consumer-biases_en (accessed on 19 September 2023). [14]

European Commission (2023), *Report from the Commission to the European Parliament and the Council on the application of Directive 2014/92/EU of the European Parliament and of the Council on the comparability of fees related to payment accounts, payment account switching and access to payment accounts with basic features*, https://eur-lex.europa.eu/legal-content/EN/TXT/?uri=COM:2023:249:FIN (accessed on 24 August 2023). [6]

European Securities and Markets Authority (2023), *Costs and Performance of EU Retail Investment Products 2023*, ESMA, https://doi.org/10.2856/720749. [1]

Financial Consumer Agency of Canada (2022), *Consumer Vulnerability: Evidence from the Monthly COVID-19 Financial Well-being Survey*, https://www.canada.ca/en/financial-consumer-agency/programs/research/consumer-vulnerability.html (accessed on 19 September 2023). [17]

Financial Services Agency (2017), *Regarding the establishment of "Principles for Customer-Oriented Business Operations"*, https://www.fsa.go.jp/news/28/20170330-1.html (accessed on 19 September 2023). [15]

FinCoNet (2021), *Financial Product Governance and Culture*, FinCoNet (International Financial Consumer Protection Organisation), http://www.finconet.org/Financial-Product-Governance-Culture.pdf (accessed on 9 August 2021). [11]

HM Treasury (2023), *Basic bank accounts: July 2021 to June 2022*, https://www.gov.uk/government/publications/basic-bank-accounts-july-2021-to-june-2022 (accessed on 25 August 2023). [9]

Hong Kong Monetary Authority, Insurance Authority and Mandatory Provident Fund Schemes Authority (2022), *Findings of Mystery Shopping Programme on Selling Practices in respect of Qualifying Deferred Annuity Policies and Tax-deductible Voluntary Contributions in Hong Kong*, https://www.hkma.gov.hk/media/eng/doc/key-information/guidelines-and-circular/2022/20221223e1.pdf (accessed on 19 September 2023). [13]

National Bank of Serbia (2022), *Decision on the payment account with basic features*, RS Official Gazette, No 89/2022, https://www.nbs.rs/export/sites/NBS_site/documents-eng/propisi/propisi-ps/platni_racun_osnovne_e.pdf (accessed on 25 August 2023). [8]

OECD (2023), "Financial consumers and sustainable finance: Policy implications and approaches", *OECD Business and Finance Policy Papers*, No. 32, OECD Publishing, Paris, https://doi.org/10.1787/318d0494-en. [10]

OECD (2022), *Dark commercial patterns*, https://www.oecd.org/digital/dark-commercial-patterns-44f5e846-en.htm (accessed on 19 September 2023). [12]

Reserve Bank of India (2014), *Basic Savings Bank Deposit Account*, https://www.rbi.org.in/commonperson/English/Scripts/FAQs.aspx?Id=1289 (accessed on 19 September 2023). [7]

Notes

[1] Insurance-based investment products (IBIPs) mix a savings component linked to market trends and fluctuations and an insurance coverage component. Some IBIPs may have guaranteed rates and others may fully or partially expose the savings component to market fluctuations (these are unit-linked products where the market risk rests on consumers).

[2] A form of price discrimination, often in insurance markets, in which new customers are offered preferential rates while long-time customers see their premiums rise repeatedly due to factors that are not linked to the risk-profile of the customer and the cost of service. EIOPA issued a supervisory statement in 2023 to address such practices across the European Union (EIOPA, 2023[18]).

5 Products and services giving rise to consumer detriment

Understanding levels of consumer detriment from specific financial products and services offered in different market sectors can help policymakers, regulators and supervisors strengthen financial consumer protection frameworks and address areas of highest concern. This chapter analyses products and services giving rise to consumer detriment in five product markets: banking and payments, credit, insurance, investments and pensions.

While the previous three chapters evaluated factors that can potentially lead to harm (i.e. risks), this chapter examines the vectors (i.e. financial products and services) through which those risks transform into actual consumer detriment. The definition of consumer detriment used for this Report is consistent with the definition provided in the OECD Recommendation on Consumer Policy Decision Making [OECD/LEGAL/0403]. The definition is as follows:

> *the harm or loss that consumers experience, when, for example, i) they are misled by unfair market practices into making purchases of goods or services that they would not have otherwise made; ii) they pay more than what they would have, had they been better informed, iii) they suffer from unfair contract terms or iv) the goods and services that they purchase do not conform to their expectations with respect to delivery or performance.*

Understanding levels of consumer detriment from specific financial products and services offered in different market sectors can help policymakers, regulators and supervisors strengthen financial consumer protection frameworks and address areas of highest concern. For each of the five market sectors (banking and payments, credit, insurance, investments, and pensions) jurisdictions were asked to select three products or services giving rise to the *most* significant consumer detriment in 2022 and indicate whether such detriment was expected to increase, decrease or stay the same in 2023.

Because quantifying consumer detriment can be challenging and definitions vary across jurisdictions, the reporting template was not overly prescriptive in how it expected jurisdictions to rank products and services. Instead, responding authorities were free to base their assessment on their knowledge of their own markets, which may be informed by consumer research, past supervisory actions, thematic reviews or complaints data, among other sources.

5.1. Banking and payments

Figure 5.1 presents banking and payment products positioned on a heatmap according to the level of consumer detriment they caused in 2022 and jurisdictions' expectations for how this level would change in 2023. The following key findings emerge:

- Transaction accounts and debit cards gave rise to the greatest consumer detriment in the banking and payments sector in 2022, primarily due to harms linked to financial scams and frauds and blocked accounts. These products were selected by 55 and 45% of respondents, respectively.[1]
- Mobile banking and digital wallets also caused concern. On average, the detriment arising from these products was expected to increase over the course of 2023 as the adoption of new digital technology may increase consumers' exposure to financial scams and frauds.
- Cross-border transactions, E-money, push payments, savings accounts and account information services gave rise to relatively less consumer detriment in 2022; however, detriment from account information services, E-money and push payments was expected to increase in 2023.
- Harm to consumers from super apps – applications that combine multiple financial and non-financial services in one platform – was expected to decrease in 2023.

Figure 5.1. Products and services giving rise to consumer detriment in the banking sector

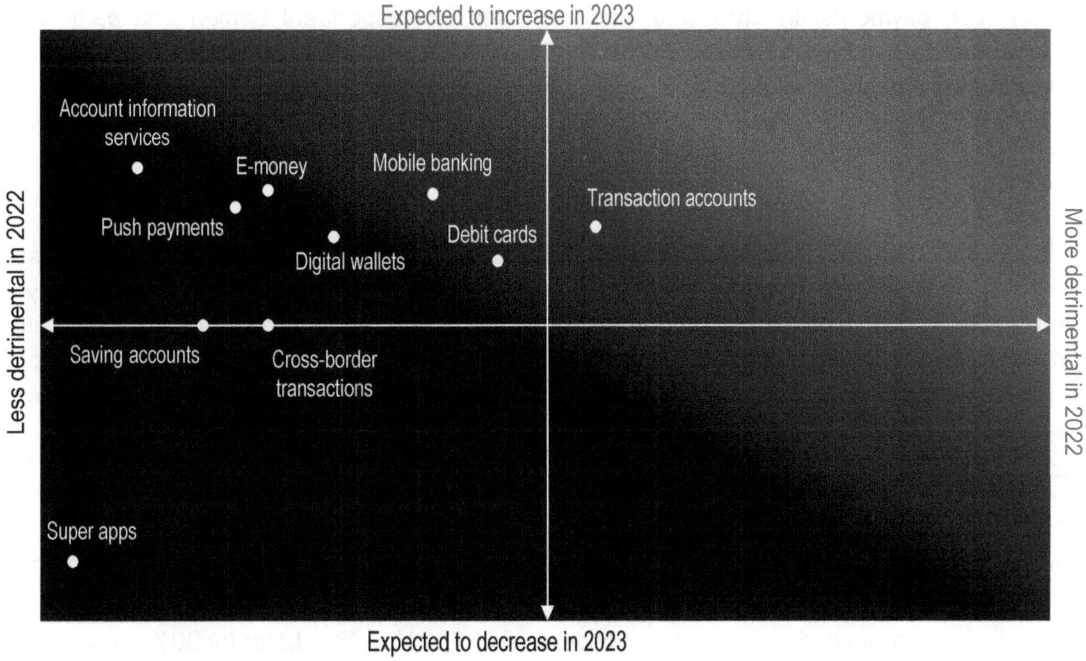

Note: The x-axis (horizontal) presents responses to questions asking for the top three products and services that gave rise to consumer detriment in the sector in 2022. The y-axis (vertical) presents responses to a follow-up question asking whether jurisdictions anticipate the detriment arising from the selected product would increase, stay the same or decrease in 2023.
Products and services are placed along the x-axis (horizontal) according to how frequently they were selected by respondents (more frequently selected products are farther to the right). The intersection of the y-axis represents the median number of responses per product, i.e., products to the right of the y-axis were selected more frequently than the median. The relative positioning of the products and services along the y-axis is determined by calculating an average of responses for the corresponding product or service ("increasing", "staying the same" or "decreasing").
Source: OECD Consumer Finance Risk Monitor Reporting Template 2023

When asked to describe the consumer detriment that could arise from banking and payment products, jurisdictions reported concerns about scams and frauds that arise from banking and payment transactions conducted online. According to a survey conducted in 2021 by the National Bank of Rwanda, around one in five Rwandan consumers reported being a victim of financial fraud. **Canada**, **Indonesia**, **Mozambique**, **Peru**, **Rwanda** and **Spain** noted that fraudsters target transaction accounts and that digital products and services come with higher potential risk of fraud to consumers. In **Bulgaria**, nearly a quarter of the complaints received by the Bulgarian National Bank concerned unauthorised payment transactions. Such scams and frauds include phishing and social engineering attacks.

Challenges can also arise related to blocked or frozen accounts. For example, in **Thailand**, contract terms may stipulate that financial service providers can freeze a customer's account if it is suspected of fraud, illegal activity, or misuse. This may, however, potentially harm consumers if there was no such activity and the freeze continues for a long period of time. **Portugal** noted that one of the most complained matters regarding deposits, including current accounts, relates to constraints imposed by the institution on the management of the account, which could include restrictions on access to the account, in particular resulting from the unavailability of digital channels, or blocking of current accounts. The **United Kingdom** described a similar phenomenon relating to firms freezing customer accounts unfairly due to a misapplication of financial crime controls. Other situations of potential detriment for the consumer include delays in closing accounts, which jeopardises consumer mobility, and difficulties opening accounts, which hampers consumers' access to indispensable banking products.

Regarding cross-border payments, **Australia** noted that a lack of transparency in the cost of conducting cross-border payments can be detrimental to consumers if they lack information and understanding about the fees on such payments. In **Lithuania**, intermediaries (correspondent banks) that participate and facilitate cross-border transactions often apply commission fees, which consumers are not made aware of before initiating the payment transaction.

5.2. Credit

Within the reporting template, the definition of credit included a range of products and services, some of which may not be legally classified as credit in certain jurisdictions but nevertheless share many of the characteristics that could be reasonably understood as credit. Such products include traditional offerings like mortgages, personal loans, credit cards and car loans. It also includes less traditional forms of credit such as payday lending, peer-to-peer lending, salary advance schemes, Buy Now Pay Later and overdraft facilities.

Figure 5.2 presents credit products and services according to the consumer detriment they caused in 2022 and jurisdictions' expectations for 2023.

- Mortgages/home loans and personal loans gave rise to the greatest consumer detriment in the credit sector in 2022; both of which were selected by 58% of respondents.[2]
- Credit cards were cited by 39% of respondents and Buy Now Pay Later by 30%. On average, the detriment arising from these products was expected to increase over the course of 2023.
- Relative to other product categories, peer-to-peer lending received the most pessimistic outlook for 2023, while the detriment arising from overdraft facilities received the least pessimistic outlook.

Figure 5.2. Products and services giving rise to consumer detriment in the credit sector

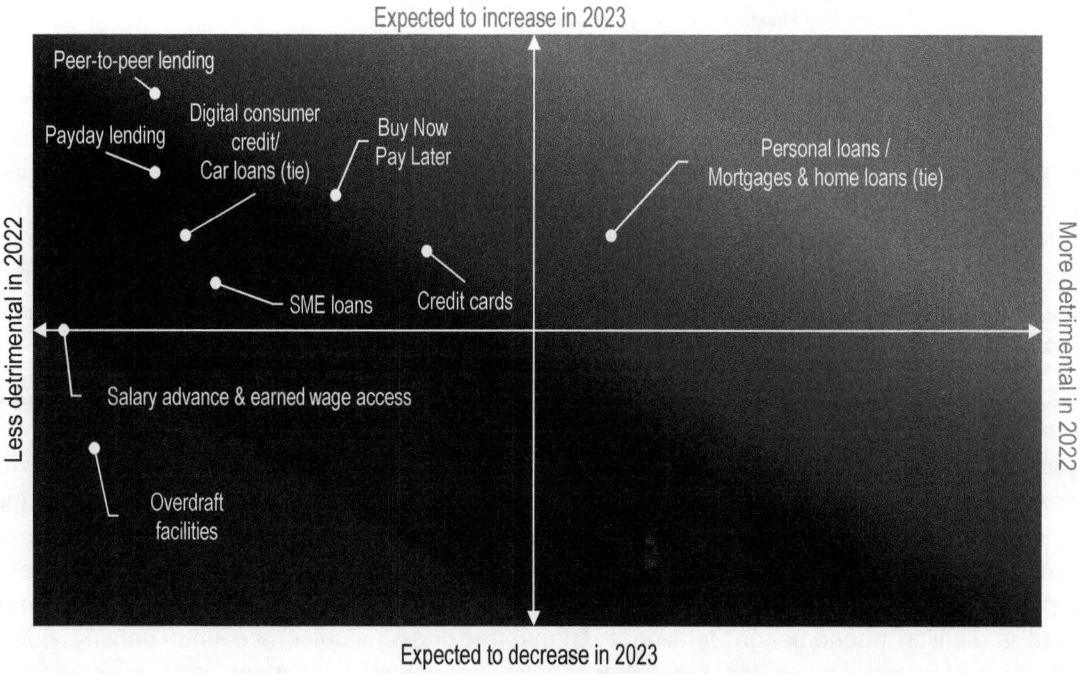

Note: The x-axis (horizontal) presents responses to questions asking for the top three products and services that gave rise to consumer detriment in the sector in 2022. The y-axis (vertical) presents responses to a follow-up question asking whether jurisdictions anticipate the detriment arising from the selected product would increase, stay the same or decrease in 2023.
Source: OECD Consumer Finance Risk Monitor Reporting Template 2023.

Regarding personal loans, consumer detriment may arise from misprocessed transactions, improper charges including unfair penalties or restrictions for earlier payback, and inadequate disclosures about the terms and conditions. **Hungary** noted the high cost of services in doorstep loans, a type of personal loan where the cash loan is delivered and collected at the home of the consumer. **Indonesia**, **Italy** and **Canada** cited debt collection practices as a cause for concern.

Interest rate hikes affected adjustable-rate mortgages held by consumers in many jurisdictions, thus increasing the debt burden on consumers and their household expenses. As shown in Figure 5.3, the share of adjustable-rate mortgages as a percentage of all mortgages issued in 2022 varied widely across jurisdictions, from 2% in the United States to 97% in Finland. This heterogeneity can be explained by demand-side factors (e.g. borrowers' preferences), supply-side factors (e.g. the types of funding available to mortgage issuers) and regulation (Albertazzi, Fringuellotti and Ongena, 2019[1]). Figure 5.3 also contrasts this proportion against mortgages issued in 2003, showing that the prevalence of adjustable-rate mortgages within jurisdictions has evolved over time, significantly increasing in **Japan** and **Canada**, for example, while falling in **Italy**, **Spain** and **Ireland**. The decline in the share of adjustable-rate mortgages in OECD countries results partly from the narrowing spread between fixed and variable rates (van Hoenselaar et al., 2021[2]).

Figure 5.3. Share of adjustable-rate mortgages issued in 2003 and 2022, in selected housing markets

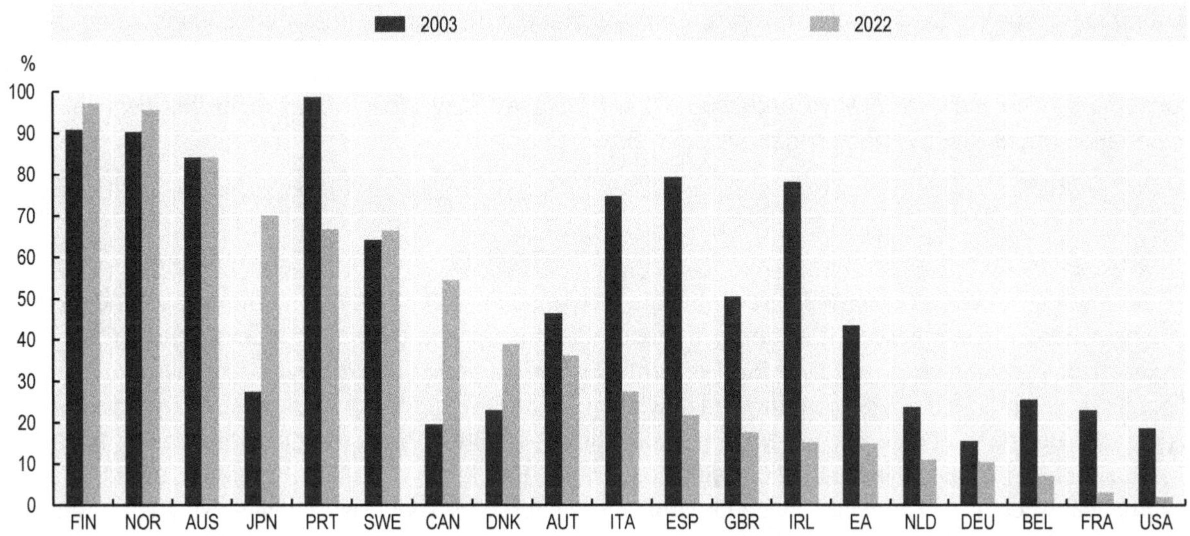

Note: Adjustable-rate mortgage loans are new loans issued at variable rate or with an initial rate fixed for a period of up to 1 year. Due to limited data availability, the light blue bars for Norway and Sweden refer to 2006. For the United Kingdom, Canada and Australia the light blue bars respectively refer to 2008, 2013 and 2019. Dark blue bars refer to 2022 or to the latest available data.
Source: ECB; Financial Conduct Authority; Japan Ministry of Land, Infrastructure, Transport and Tourism; Norges Bank; Federal Housing Finance Agency; Bank of Canada; Australian Bureau of Statistics, and OECD calculations published in OECD (2022[3]), *OECD Economic Outlook, Volume 2022 Issue 2.*

The Financial Consumer Agency of **Canada** noted data points and anecdotal examples suggesting that variable rate mortgages with fixed payments were most likely sold to consumers who did not understand the product or would have not qualified for other types of mortgages at the time of application. FCAC concluded that this specific product, although attractive in a low interest rate setting, offers poor value to consumers when interest rates start rising rapidly. To address this growing concern and the increase of financial hardship consumers are facing, FCAC published industry guidelines in 2023 on its expectations for how banks should handle existing consumer mortgage loans in exceptional circumstances (Financial Consumer Agency of Canada, 2023[4]).

In **Luxembourg**, 40% of outstanding mortgage loans have variable interest rates, meaning that consumers who hold these mortgages in their jurisdictions are at increased risk of vulnerability with interest rate hikes. The Commission de Surveillance du Secteur Financier (CSSF) therefore has requested banks to perform an interest rate sensitivity analysis at loan origination to improve consumer protection in the future. Similarly in **Slovak Republic,** lenders are required to "stress test" applications in line with the National Bank of the Slovak Republic's regulatory limit on the debt-to-income ratio of loan applicants. **Portugal** approved in 2022 a set of temporary rules to mitigate the impact of the increase of interest rates in mortgage credit contracts with variable interest rates and to assist borrowers at risk of default due to increased rates. Under these measures, lenders are bound to carry out an assessment of the borrower's capacity. In case the borrower's debt service-to-income ratio is significantly affected by the increase of interest rate, lenders must propose various solutions including the consolidation of several credit agreements or a new credit agreement to refinance the debt, an extension of the repayment period, the application of a grace period, the deferral of part of the capital or a temporary reduction in the interest rate. Portuguese authorities also approved the temporary suspension of the early repayment fee for variable rate mortgage credit regardless of the amount of the outstanding debt. Additional temporary measures were introduced in October 2023 through which certain homeowners can request that their bank reduce the loan's underlying benchmark (six-month Euribor) by 30% over two years, deferring principal to a later stage.

The **United States** also noted that interest rate hikes coupled with price increases in the auto sector led to a rapid increase in the size of auto loans, changes that put pressure on many consumers' budgets.

A number of jurisdictions noted that Buy Now Pay Later (BNPL) schemes risk over-indebtedness for consumers, who may not always understand the risks they may incur when using this service. More information about BNPL schemes is provided in Box 5.1.

Box 5.1. Buy Now Pay Later

Buy Now Pay Later has emerged in recent years as a popular method of making purchases and paying in instalments. In some ways it is simply a modern iteration of the type of consumer lending that has existed for years, growing notably in the 19th century when it helped bring relatively expensive consumer goods (e.g. furniture, farm equipment, and sewing machines) within reach of people on limited incomes (Harvard Business School, n.d.[5]). More recently, however, BNPL has emerged as a distinct financial product, driven in part by increased digitalisation. Today, BNPL is a global phenomenon, a widely used and easily accessible financial service for consumers offered by specialised entities such as Afterpay, Klarna and Affirm as well as BigTechs including Apple (via MasterCard and Goldman Sachs) and Amazon (via Affirm). Uptake of the product increased dramatically in recent years in many jurisdictions. In the **United States**, the volume of BNPL loans increased twelvefold between 2019 and 2021 (Consumer Financial Protection Bureau, 2022[6]). In the **United Kingdom**, the value of transactions using BNPL nearly quadrupled between January and December 2020 (Financial Conduct Authority, 2021[7]), with a 2023 survey revealing that 27% of UK adults had used such products in the prior six months (Financial Conduct Authority, 2023[8]). Globally, the BNPL market is estimated to continue growing at a compound annual growth rate of 26.1% from 2023 to 2030, when it is expected to reach nearly USD 40 billion (Grand View Research, 2022[9]).

While BNPL products are clearly popular with consumers and appear to be filling a need in the market, policymakers, regulators and supervisors around the world are increasingly concerned about the potential consumer harms arising from BNPL products and the limitations of existing policy frameworks to adequately protect consumers from over-commitment in terms of their repayment obligations.

Indeed, of the 43 jurisdictions participating in the 2023 OECD Consumer Finance Risk Monitor, nearly one in three mentioned BNPL as an area of concern or of future regulatory action.

Jurisdictions are particularly concerned about the increasing use of BNPL among consumers who may already be struggling financially due to rising inflation, depressed incomes and increasing interest rates, therefore increasing the risk of over-indebtedness. The Central Bank of **Malaysia**, for example, expressed concerns that consumers may be more susceptible to unfair treatment and accumulation of excessive debt due to the proliferation of credit providers who sometimes fall outside the regulator's reach. In the current economic context, the relative ease of access to BNPL facilities can place users at a higher risk of spending beyond their means, without considering their ability to repay the full amount. The **Netherlands** shared this concern, noting that while the risk does not pertain to most users engaging with the product, the most significant danger posed by BNPL is its potential contribution to over-indebtedness for consumers in an already vulnerable financial situation. According to research from the **United States**, BNPL users have lower credit scores and are more likely to be in financial distress than other consumers.

Authorities are also concerned about the lack of transparency regarding fees and charges, particularly for late payments. The Central Bank of **Malaysia**, citing anecdotal evidence among selected larger BNPL players in the market, noted an increasing trend in missed repayments, suggesting that such risks may be rising. Authorities from **Germany** and **Ireland** expressed concerns about consumers, especially youth, not understanding the underlying construct and potential repercussions of using BNPL products. Beyond the lack of transparency and disclosure of information to consumers, authorities from **Italy,** the **Netherlands** and **Portugal** further cited poor creditworthiness assessments as an additional risk, as well as aggressive marketing that promotes impulse buying. In addition to the lack of robust creditworthiness assessments, the use of BNPL products does not appear on credit reports in the **United States**, raising potential systemic risk concerns.

BNPL facilities are not always regulated or subject to the same rules as other forms of credit due to certain features of the product (e.g. amount borrowed, number of instalments, lack of interest charges). In some jurisdictions, the regulatory framework for credit – and the associated protections – only applies in certain cases, depending on the specific design of the service. Notwithstanding the legal status of BNPL vis-à-vis jurisdictional definitions of credit, the risks posed to consumers are much the same.

To respond to the growth of BNPL and the related risks, policymakers and supervisory authorities have launched a range of actions and initiatives, including consumer research, awareness campaigns, self-regulation, and the introduction of new legislation and regulation.

- In May 2023, the Minister for Financial Services of **Australia** announced intentions to regulate BNPL as a form of credit under the National Consumer Credit Protection Act 2009 (Credit Act). This regulation would include new requirements for BNPL providers, including product disclosures, affordability assessments, fee caps, credit records and licensing obligations among others.
- In 2023, **Finland** amended its Consumer Protection Act which, among other things, introduced stipulations regarding the presentation of available payment methods online. The amendments prohibit online retailers from setting any payment method as a default choice. Further, the amended Act requires retailers to order the presentation of payment methods with payments-in-full first (i.e. immediate debits), followed by card payments and mobile payments second, and lastly any methods that involve deferrals, instalments or applying for credit (which would include BNPL).
- Consumer research by the Competition and Consumer Protection Commission in **Ireland** found that 'not borrowing for daily expenses' is one of the two key behaviours that directly affects financial well-being. Given BNPL's availability, how convenient it is and how tempting it is for

consumers, Irish authorities are concerned that this will have a negative impact on consumers financial well-being. BNPL is regulated by the Central Bank, but agreements under EUR 500 (Euro area euros) and certain agreements over EUR 500, where interest is not charged, are not reported into the Central Credit Register, which means that other lenders may not have a full picture of the debt a consumer has when they assess their creditworthiness and could lead to over-indebtedness. The Competition and Consumer Protection Commission of Ireland launched a BNPL campaign targeting younger consumers aged 18 to 35. It created two videos, one which explained BNPL to consumers and another focused on the potential for hidden costs with this type of credit arrangement. It used the main social media platforms to promote the videos, with the addition of Snapchat and TikTok, to reach the target audience.

- The Bank of **Italy** undertook an in-depth evaluation on BNPL schemes, noting that a common BNPL scheme in Italy is one where the deferment is formally granted by the seller, who immediately after (or even at the same time as the transaction) assigns the credit to a specialised intermediary, based on former agreements. Bank of Italy subsequently issued a public warning to increase overall awareness among consumers on the risks they may incur in relation to such credit facilities (e.g. exposure to over-indebtedness due to poor creditworthiness assessment procedures). The communication drew consumers' attention to potential risks and to the safeguards provided by the regulatory framework protecting bank customers.
- In the **Netherlands**, the Autoriteit Financiele Markten (AFM) published a large study on BNPL in 2022, noting that while the product may provide flexibility for consumers and increase sales for online shops, it also posed risks for financially vulnerable consumers and contribute to debt accumulation. Further, it could lead to debt habituation, which they defined as the normalisation of buying on credit. The study emphasised that BNPL providers were not obligated to perform robust creditworthiness checks. In conclusion, the AFM voiced its support for proposals to revise the European Consumer Credit Directive, which would introduce various requirements for BNPL providers and allow AFM to supervise the provision of such products.
- The Banco de **Portugal** reported closely monitoring the expansion of BNPL products in the consumer credit sector, anticipating over-indebtedness and default. Portugal also noted that while consumer credit under EUR 200 was not subject to regulatory requirements, the revision of the EU Consumer Credit Directive will bring BNPL products within the scope of the Directive, which will be reflected in the Portuguese framework.
- The Monetary Authority of **Singapore** (MAS) determined that an industry code (as opposed to regulations) would be a risk-proportionate response to BNPL-related developments, which remains a very small segment compared to other means of consumer payments. The code, launched in November 2022, seeks to protect consumers' interests by formalising safeguards such as no compounding interest, a cap on late fees, clear disclosures and fair marketing, suspension of account upon customer delinquency and a requirement for BNPL firms to conduct additional creditworthiness assessments before exceeding a stipulated credit cap with the provider. MAS noted that they would continue to monitor the industry's implementation of the safeguards set out in the Code and continue to work with the industry to mitigate the risk of consumer over-indebtedness.
- In February 2021, the **United Kingdom** government announced its intention to regulate interest-free BNPL products. The government consulted on policy options to deliver a proportionate approach to regulation in October 2021, followed by a consultation response in June 2022. The government subsequently consulted on a proposed draft legislation that would bring BNPL into Financial Conduct Authority regulation.

The policy and regulatory challenges raised by BNPL will feed into and be reflected in the upcoming assessment of the OECD Recommendation on Consumer Protection in the field of Consumer Credit

[OECD/LEGAL/0453], which is the only global standard on consumer credit. The Recommendation, first adopted in 1977 and updated in 2019, sets out high-level recommendations for Adherents to take measures relating to the protection of consumers in the context of consumer credit transactions. The G20/OECD Task Force on Financial Consumer Protection has responsibility for overseeing the implementation of the Recommendation and ensuring that it remains up to date. Given the importance of BNPL on the policy agenda of regulators globally, the review of the Recommendation will necessarily include a close assessment of any modifications that the BNPL trend may require.

5.3. Insurance

Figure 5.4 presents insurance products and services according to the consumer detriment they caused in 2022 and jurisdictions' expectations for 2023.

- Selected by over half of respondents, motor and life insurance gave rise to the greatest consumer detriment in the insurance sector in 2022.[3]
- Credit protection and health insurance were also cited by 36% of respondents.
- The detriment arising from life, credit protection and health insurance was expected to increase over the course of 2023, while harms from motor insurance were expected to remain the same.
- Relatively few jurisdictions ranked travel and gadget insurance among the top products causing detriment in 2022; however, jurisdictions anticipated that the harm arising from travel and gadget insurance would increase in 2023.

Figure 5.4. Products and services giving rise to consumer detriment in the insurance sector

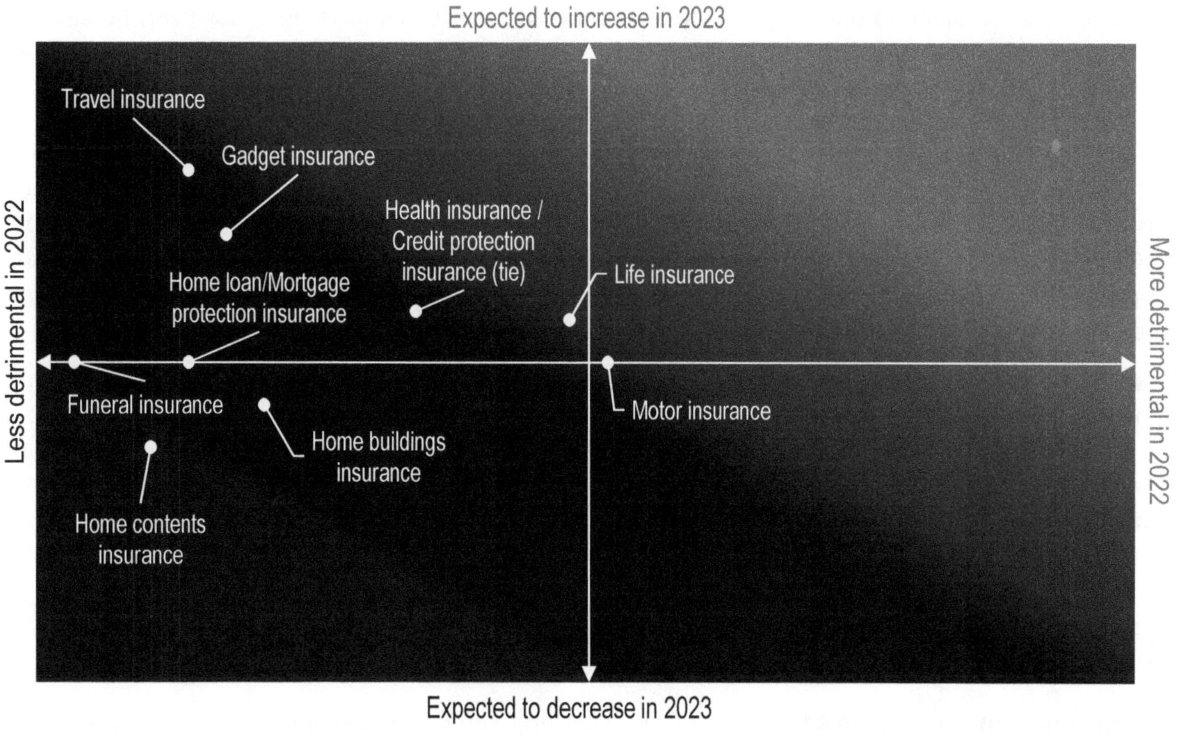

Note: The x-axis (horizontal) presents responses to questions asking for the top three products and services that gave rise to consumer detriment in the sector in 2022. The y-axis (vertical) presents responses to a follow-up question asking whether jurisdictions anticipate the detriment arising from the selected product would increase, stay the same or decrease in 2023.
Source: OECD Consumer Finance Risk Monitor Reporting Template 2023.

Additionally, jurisdictions mentioned certain business practices, such as bundling or tying products, which in certain instances risk causing consumer detriment in the insurance sector. **Austria, Luxembourg**, and **Romania** noted that the business models for the sale of insurance products can often be the main cause of consumer detriment. Such business models may be designed to generate revenue in the form of commission payments for the party distributing these products, which can result in products being sold that offer limited value to the consumer. In addition, as noted by **South Africa**, products are often bundled or linked with other products which may lead to confusion or misunderstanding among consumers if there are not effective disclosures and transparency about the products.

In an example from the **United Kingdom**, Guaranteed Asset Protection (GAP) insurance is an add-on insurance product sold by non-regulated entities alongside the purchase of another product (generally motor vehicles). In its research into the sector, the Financial Conduct Authority found that it was characterised by high levels of commissions paid to the distributors, alongside extremely low claims frequencies. In **France**, affinity or add-on insurance products have given rise to numerous complaints from consumers. In response, the Financial Sector Advisory Committee unanimously adopted an opinion to strengthen consumer protection relating to this product. The opinion addresses the collection of the policyholder's consent, provision of annual information and clarification that the consumer is signing an insurance contract and not a legal or commercial warranty.

Unit-linked products can lead to much confusion or misinterpretation, for instance consumers who purchase investment-linked policies (ILPs) may not adequately understand the product features. Additionally, credit protection insurance (CPI) may cause consumer detriment when the cost of bundled CPI is higher than what the actual loss ratio would suggest. Consumers are also sometimes unaware that they have purchased CPI. In Europe, tying (where banks require borrowers to purchase a CPI when taking out a loan) is generally prohibited under the Mortgage Credit Directive, but a thematic review conducted by EIOPA revealed that such practices remain widespread (EIOPA, 2022[10]). In **Peru**, financial institutions are similarly forbidden to force clients to purchase credit life insurance offered by them, and insurance companies are forbidden to bundle credit life insurance with additional coverage. However, in the digital environment, new concerning practices have emerged, particularly with regard to credit or debit card insurance (CCI), where insurance providers consider the fraud coverage in digital/online environments as an additional coverage with an extra charge; a product design that the SBS notes is not aligned with the current trend of increasing digital transactions. In **Chile**, the practice of bundling credit protection insurance products with consumer credit is widespread. While not always an unfair practice, it can often cause consumer detriment, especially if consumers purchase insurance that they do not want or need. In 2021, the Chilean Consumer Protection Authority (SERNAC) entered into a settlement with several insurance companies regarding mis-selling of insurance with retail store credit cards that consumers were not aware of purchasing.

Jurisdictions also mentioned that for many of these products, there is uncertainty or confusion around what is covered and what is not, especially with regards to gadget insurance and travel insurance. Jurisdictions also noted high levels of dissatisfaction among consumers generally regarding claims compensations and claims handling and that delays in compensation could be particularly pronounced with motor insurance. In **the Netherlands**, consumer detriment also arises from uninsurable losses due to climate change and natural hazards (see Box 2.1 in Chapter 2 for more information on natural hazards).

5.4. Investments

The reporting template presented a range of products and services under the category of investments. Examples include managed funds, equity, fixed income products, derivatives trading, financial advice, sustainable finance, and retail/self-direct online investment platforms. Digital assets, including crypto-assets, were included as a type of investment product, even though they may not be treated as regulated investments in many jurisdictions. Figure 5.5 presents investments products and services according to the consumer detriment they caused in 2022 and jurisdictions' expectations for 2023:

- More than half of respondents selected cryptocurrencies and digital assets as giving rise to the greatest consumer detriment in the investments sector in 2022, whereas the next most frequently selected product and service (derivatives trading) was only selected by around a third of respondents.[4]
- Overall, jurisdictions expected that the harm from cryptocurrencies and digital assets would increase in 2023 along with detriment from retail/self-directed online investments, equity and sustainable financial products.
- Detriment from fixed income and unit-linked insurance was expected to remain the same in 2023.
- Consumer detriment arising from derivatives trading, financial advisory services and managed funds was expected to decrease in 2023.

Figure 5.5. Products and services giving rise to consumer detriment in the investments sector

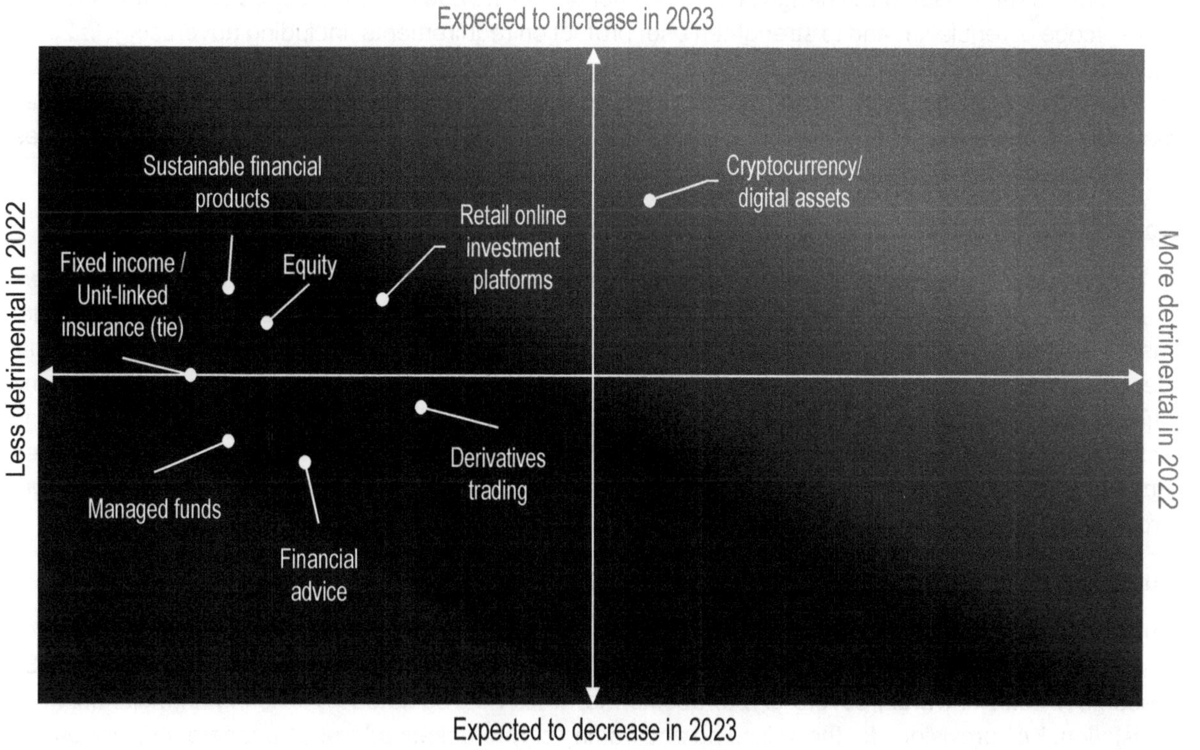

Note: The x-axis (horizontal) presents responses to questions asking for the top three products and services that gave rise to consumer detriment in the sector in 2022. The y-axis (vertical) presents responses to a follow-up question asking whether jurisdictions anticipate the detriment arising from the selected product would increase, stay the same or decrease in 2023.
Source: OECD Consumer Finance Risk Monitor Reporting Template 2023.

Jurisdictions indicated that digital assets, including crypto-assets, give rise to consumer detriment given their highly volatile nature. In some jurisdictions, crypto-asset activities are unregulated, though this is changing (see Box 5.2 below for more detail); in other jurisdictions, crypto-asset activities are conducted in non-compliance with applicable domestic regulations (OECD, 2022[11]; OECD, 2022[12]). Research in **the Netherlands** shows that 1 in 10 crypto-asset users engage with high-risk leveraged strategies involving crypto-assets. In **Ontario, Canada**, retail investor participation in capital markets rapidly grew during the pandemic; for some self-directed investors, a desire for returns in the face of challenging and uncertain macro-economic conditions may have led to more speculative investments in crypto-assets. Furthermore, retail investors face risks connected with trading decisions based on informal recommendations via social networks and unregulated online platforms from outside Canada, which may provide misleading information or information without proper risk warnings.

Box 5.2. Recent developments in regulating crypto-assets

In the last several years, jurisdictions around the world have clarified, strengthened or introduced regulations pertaining to crypto-assets. Four examples are set out below.

Japan: Three successive legal reforms

Japan first began reforming their crypto-asset regulatory framework in 2016, when a registration system was introduced for crypto-asset exchange service providers. The system requires identity verification upon account openings and uses a framework for user protection including minimum capital requirements, disclosure and segregation of assets. In 2019, the Payment Services Act and the Financial Instruments and Exchange Act were amended to include crypto-asset derivative transactions in the scope of regulation and to strengthen user protection requirements, including advertising. In 2022, the third legal reform amended the Banking Act, the Payment Services Act and the Trust Business Act to introduce a regulatory framework with banks, fund transfer service providers and trust companies as issuers of stablecoins. The reforms also introduced a registration system for stablecoin intermediaries (Financial Services Agency, 2022[13]).

South Africa: Declaration of a Crypto-Asset as a Financial Product

In October 2022, the Financial Sector Conduct Authority of South Africa published in the *Government Gazette* and on its website a Declaration of a Crypto-Asset as a Financial Product (Declaration) under the Financial Advisory and Intermediary Services Act, 2002 (Act No. 37 of 2002) (FAIS Act) (Financial Sector Conduct Authority, 2022[14]). The FSCA also released a Policy Document providing clarity on the effect of the Declaration, including transitional provisions, and the approach the FSCA would take in establishing a regulatory and licensing framework that would be applicable to Financial Services Providers (FSPs) that provide financial services in relation to crypto-assets. The declaration brought providers of financial services in relation to crypto-assets within the FSCA's regulatory jurisdiction.

European Union: Markets in Crypto-assets (MiCA) Regulation

The Markets in Crypto-Assets Regulation (MiCA) introduced market rules for crypto-assets in the European Union. The regulation, which entered into force in June 2023 and will be applicable from 30 December 2024 onwards, covers crypto-assets that were not regulated by existing financial services legislation. Key provisions for those issuing and trading crypto-assets address transparency, disclosure, authorisation and supervision of transactions. The new legal framework will support market integrity and financial stability by regulating public offers of crypto-assets and by ensuring consumers are better informed about their associated risks (European Parliament and Council of the European Union, 2023[15]).

Financial Stability Board (FSB) Global Regulatory Framework for Crypto-asset Activities and Global Stablecoins

In July of 2023 the FSB published its Global Regulatory Framework for Crypto-asset Activities to promote consistency and co-ordination of regulatory and supervisory approaches regarding crypto-assets. This Framework comprises two sets of recommendations. The first consists of high-level recommendations for the regulation, supervision and oversight of crypto-asset activities, and the second concerns recommendations for the regulation, supervision and oversight of global stablecoin arrangements. These recommendations are based on the principle of "same activity, same risk, same regulation" to promote high-level, flexible and technology-neutral recommendations to ensure crypto-asset activities and stablecoins are subject to consistent and comprehensive regulation corresponding to the risks they pose, while also supporting innovation from technological advances.

In addition to crypto-assets, **Italy** noted that potential detriment arises from the complexity and riskiness of derivatives trading that consumers may not easily understand. In terms of financial advice, countries and jurisdictions point to the average consumer getting investment "advice" from social media and not professional financial advisors. Indeed, a survey of investors in **Brazil** (average age of 32) revealed that around 75% of respondents began investing based on information from YouTube channels and influencers (Comissão de Valores Mobiliários, 2023[16]). **Slovak Republic** noted that this risk may be exacerbated among consumers with low levels of financial literacy.

Portugal noted that investors seemed to be making their own investments via self-directed platforms, often boosted by advice from digital influencers (who sometimes lack proper financial literacy). Simultaneously, the so-called zero commission platforms generate a lot of interest, especially with new investors who do not fully realise that "there are no free lunches", and therefore are paying commissions indirectly with the additional risk of derailing their investment objectives.

Australia, **Chile**, **Italy**, **Portugal**, **Romania**, **Slovenia** and **Spain** also mentioned that as consumer demand for sustainable finance grows, there is a potential greenwashing risk as marketing of these new products can be misleading to potential investors.

5.5. Pensions

Figure 5.6 presents pensions products and services according to the consumer detriment they caused in 2022 and jurisdictions' expectations for 2023.

- Benefits payments and management of assets gave rise to the greatest consumer detriment in the pensions sector in 2022.
- The harm arising from issues related to benefits payments, however, was expected to decrease in 2023.
- On the contrary, jurisdictions expected that harms related to financial advice and the provision of information would stay the same or increase in 2023.

Figure 5.6. Products and services giving rise to consumer detriment in the pensions sector

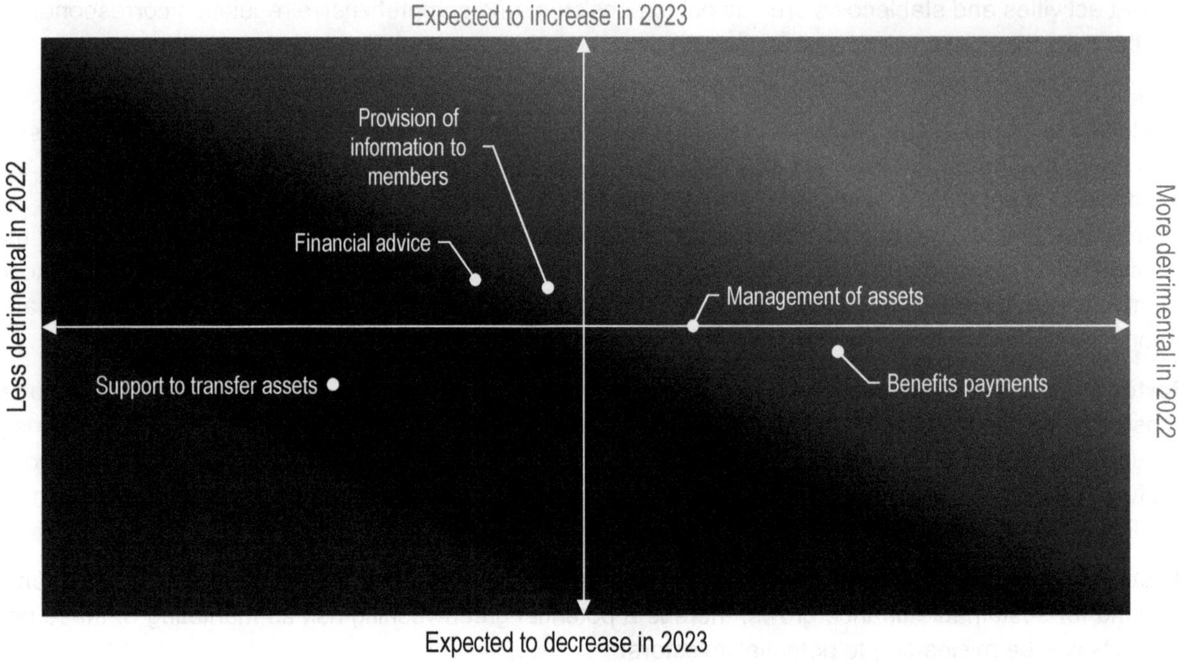

Note: The x-axis (horizontal) presents responses to questions asking for the top three products and services that gave rise to consumer detriment in the sector in 2022. The y-axis (vertical) presents responses to a follow-up question asking whether jurisdictions anticipate the detriment arising from the selected product would increase, stay the same or decrease in 2023.
Source: OECD Consumer Finance Risk Monitor Reporting Template 2023.

Regarding benefits payments, many jurisdictions cited delays in payments and concerns that payments from Defined Benefit schemes would be low unless adjusted for inflation. In terms of management of assets, **Hong Kong (China)** and **Rwanda** noted that some consumers feel they do not have adequate knowledge or experience on pension funds management; furthermore, consumers who do not have much investment knowledge or experience may not be able to choose products that best match their outcome expectations and risk appetites (OECD, 2020[17]). **Sweden** described how commission structures may also create incentives for the distributor to persuade consumers to purchase a product with a high commission, even if the product is not suitable for that customer.

Jurisdictions also noted how increased market volatility had led some pension funds to underperform; people were also permitted to make early withdrawals, which then could cause problems later when they retire. In **Hungary**, the annual returns in 2022 fell short of the defined Reference Yields. Assets earmarked for retirement fell in most OECD countries in 2022, with the value of these plans falling by 14% compared to 2021 (OECD, 2023[18]) – the largest decrease since the 2008 global financial crisis. Outside of the OECD, pension assets rose in 27 of 40 jurisdictions reporting data to the OECD, with an aggregate growth of 3.8%.

References

Albertazzi, U., F. Fringuellotti and S. Ongena (2019), "Fixed rate versus adjustable rate mortgages: evidence from euro area banks", No. 2322, European Central Bank, https://doi.org/10.2866/895495. [1]

Comissão de Valores Mobiliários (2023), *CVM divulga estudo sobre possível regulamentação envolvendo influenciadores digitais e o mercado de capitais — Comissão de Valores Mobiliários*, https://www.gov.br/cvm/pt-br/assuntos/noticias/cvm-divulga-estudo-sobre-possivel-regulamentacao-envolvendo-influenciadores-digitais-e-o-mercado-de-capitais (accessed on 10 August 2023). [16]

Consumer Financial Protection Bureau (2022), *Buy Now, Pay Later: Market trends and consumer impacts*, https://s3.amazonaws.com/files.consumerfinance.gov/f/documents/cfpb_buy-now-pay-later-market-trends-consumer-impacts_report_2022-09.pdf (accessed on 25 August 2023). [6]

EIOPA (2022), *Thematic Review on Credit Protection Insurance (CPI) sold via banks*, https://www.eiopa.europa.eu/publications/thematic-review-credit-protection-insurance-cpi-sold-banks_en (accessed on 20 September 2023). [10]

European Parliament and Council of the European Union (2023), *Regulation (EU) 2023/1114 of the European Parliament and of the Council of 31 May 2023 on markets in crypto-assets, and amending Regulations (EU) No 1093/2010 and (EU) No 1095/2010 and Directives 2013/36/EU and (EU) 2019/1937*, https://eur-lex.europa.eu/legal-content/EN/TXT/?uri=CELEX%3A32023R1114&pk_campaign=todays_OJ&pk_source=EURLEX&pk_medium=TW&pk_keyword=Crypto%20assets&pk_content=Regulation&pk_cid=EURLEX_todaysOJ (accessed on 25 August 2023). [15]

Financial Conduct Authority (2023), *Financial Lives January 2023*, https://www.fca.org.uk/publications/financial-lives/financial-lives-january-2023-consumer-experience (accessed on 8 November 2023). [8]

Financial Conduct Authority (2021), *The Woolard Review: A review of change and innovation in the unsecured credit market*, https://www.fca.org.uk/publication/corporate/woolard-review-report.pdf (accessed on 25 August 2023). [7]

Financial Consumer Agency of Canada (2023), *Guideline on Existing Consumer Mortgage Loans in Exceptional Circumstances*, https://www.canada.ca/en/financial-consumer-agency/services/industry/commissioner-guidance/mortgage-loans-exceptional-circumstances.html (accessed on 27 September 2023). [4]

Financial Sector Conduct Authority (2022), "Declaration of a Crypto Asset as a Financial Product under the Financial Advisory and Intermediary Services Act, 2002", https://www.fsca.co.za/Regulatory%20Frameworks/Temp/Policy%20Document%20supporting%20the%20Declaration%20of%20crypto%20assets%20as%20a%20financial%20product.pdf (accessed on 25 August 2023). [14]

Financial Services Agency (2022), *Regulating the crypto assets landscape in Japan*, https://www.fsa.go.jp/en/news/2022/20221207/01.pdf (accessed on 25 August 2023). [13]

Grand View Research (2022), *Buy Now Pay Later Market Size & Share Report, 2030*, https://www.grandviewresearch.com/industry-analysis/buy-now-pay-later-market-report (accessed on 25 August 2023). [9]

Harvard Business School (n.d.), *Buy Now, Pay Later: A History of Personal Credit*, Baker Library Historical Collections, https://www.library.hbs.edu/hc/credit/credit1a.html (accessed on 10 August 2023). [5]

OECD (2023), *Pension Markets in Focus 2023*, OECD Publishing, Paris, https://doi.org/10.1787/28970baf-en. [18]

OECD (2022), "Lessons from the crypto winter: DeFi versus CeFi", *OECD Business and Finance Policy Papers*, No. 18, OECD Publishing, Paris, https://doi.org/10.1787/199edf4f-en. [12]

OECD (2022), *OECD Economic Outlook, Volume 2022 Issue 2*, OECD Publishing, Paris, https://doi.org/10.1787/f6da2159-en. [3]

OECD (2022), *Why Decentralised Finance (DeFi) Matters and the Policy Implications*, OECD, Paris. [11]

OECD (2020), *OECD Pensions Outlook 2020*, OECD Publishing, Paris, https://doi.org/10.1787/67ede41b-en. [17]

van Hoenselaar, F. et al. (2021), "Mortgage finance across OECD countries", *OECD Economics Department Working Papers*, No. 1693, OECD Publishing, Paris, https://doi.org/10.1787/f97d7fe0-en. [2]

Notes

[1] Percentages are calculated based on the number of respondents who provided answers to this question (N=31).

[2] Percentages are calculated based on the number of respondents who provided answers to this question (N=33).

[3] Percentages are calculated based on the number of respondents who provided answers to this question (N=28)

[4] Percentage is calculated based on the number of respondents who provided answers to this question (N=29).

6 Consumer complaints

Data gathered through consumer complaints about financial products and services can signal gaps in financial consumer protection frameworks and highlight areas that may need to be addressed by policymakers and regulatory and supervisory authorities tasked with administering and enforcing financial consumer protection laws, regulations and other measures. This chapter reports data on consumer complaints in five product markets: banking and payments, credit, insurance, investments and pensions.

An important component of financial consumer protection frameworks are accessible and efficient recourse mechanisms that address and resolve consumer complaints. Principle 12 of the G20/OECD High-Level Principles on Financial Consumer Protection notes that financial services providers and intermediaries should have in place mechanisms for complaints handling and redress. In instances where complaints are not resolved by the internal dispute resolutions mechanisms of providers and intermediaries, consumers should have access to an independent redress process. Finally, the Principle recommends that aggregate information on consumer complaints and their resolutions should be made public.

Data gathered through consumer complaints about financial products and services can signal gaps in financial consumer protection frameworks and highlight areas that may need to be addressed by policymakers and regulatory and supervisory authorities tasked with administering and enforcing financial consumer protection laws, regulations and other measures. At the same time, complaints data are not fully representative of all consumers, since socio-economic characteristics and personality traits may make certain consumers more likely than others to file complaints (CGAP, 2022[1]). Furthermore, a rise in the volume of complaints does not necessarily indicate an increase in consumer detriment. It can also signal greater consumer awareness of the complaints and redress mechanisms available to them or a strengthened trust in the efficacy of such systems.

The reporting template surveyed jurisdictions about the top five subjects of consumer complaints in five product markets: banking and payments, credit, insurance, investments and pensions. The complaints data were further categorised by the recipient of the complaint: firms, alternative dispute resolution schemes (ADR) and supervisory authorities.

This chapter first presents aggregate trends in the volume of consumer complaints received by firms, ADR schemes and supervisory authorities from 2021 to 2022. Next, the chapter discusses the top five subjects of consumer complaints in each of the five product markets. It should be noted that in most jurisdictions, consumers are required or encouraged to initially file a complaint directly with their financial service provider (i.e. firms). If the issue is not resolved, then the consumer can escalate the problem to an ADR scheme or in certain cases to a supervisory authority. In some jurisdictions, consumers can file complaints directly with the supervisory authority as well. Finally, for the sake of simplicity, the reporting template collected data on the subject of complaints (i.e. what went wrong) rather than the specific product or type of provider involved.

6.1. Aggregate trends in consumer complaints

The total volume of consumer complaints increased in the majority of reporting jurisdictions in 2022 compared to 2021, as shown in Figure 6.1. In around three quarters of responding jurisdictions, complaints filed directly with firms or with alternative dispute resolution mechanisms increased. Complaints filed with supervisory authorities increased in a slightly lower share of jurisdictions: around 60%. The remainder of this chapter provides detailed data on trends in consumer complaints in each sector.

Figure 6.1. Total volume of complaints

Percentage of jurisdictions reporting that complaints had increased, stayed the same or decreased from 2021 to 2022, by recipient of complaint

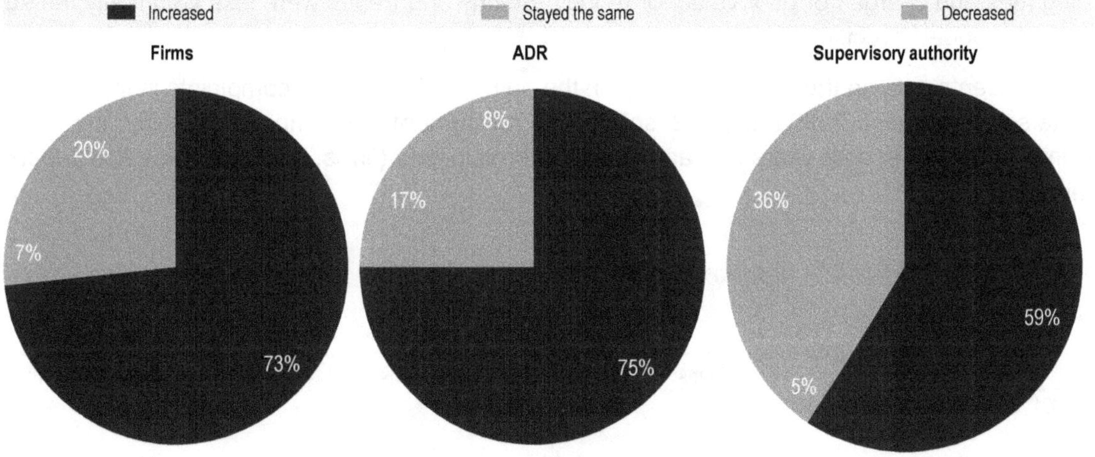

Notes: Data was provided in response to a question asking jurisdictions to indicate whether the total number of complaints received from consumers (across all products and sectors regulated) increased, stayed the same or decreased in 2022 compared to 2021. For this question, 15 jurisdictions provided an answer regarding complaints received by firms, 12 regarding complaints received by ADR mechanisms, and 22 regarding complaints received by supervisory authorities.
Source: OECD Consumer Finance Risk Monitor Reporting Template 2023.

6.2. Banking and payments

Figure 6.2. Top five subjects of consumer complaints in the banking and payments sector, by recipient of complaint

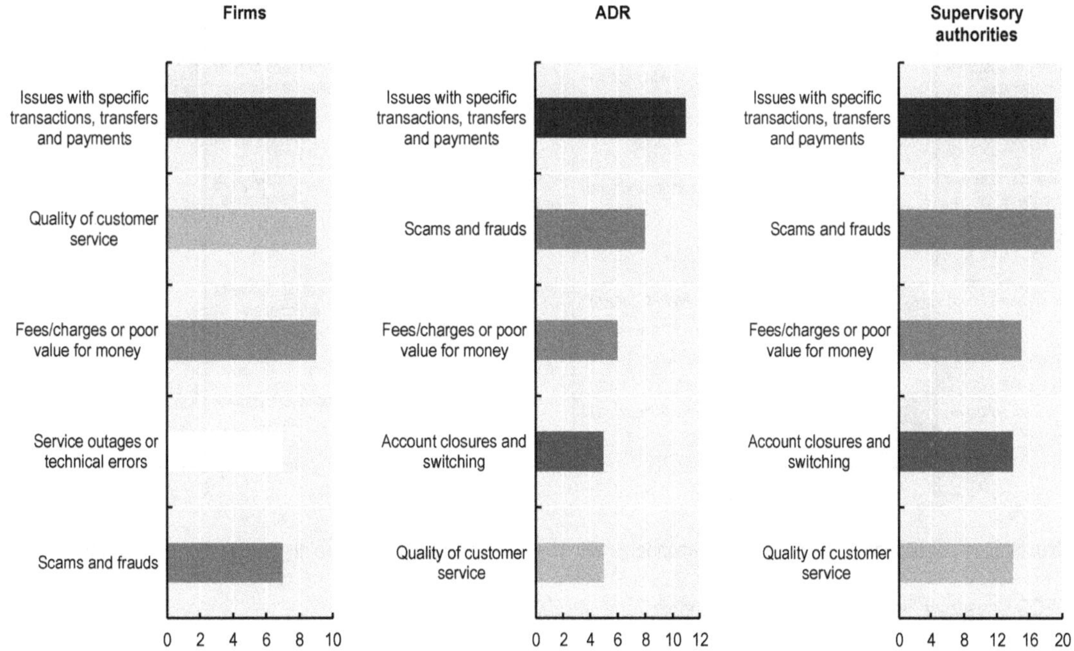

Note: Horizontal bars correspond to the number of respondents who ranked this subject of complaints among the top five in their jurisdiction in 2022.
Source: OECD Consumer Finance Risk Monitor Reporting Template 2023.

As shown in Figure 6.2, across firms, ADR schemes and supervisory authorities in the banking and payments sector, the most common subject of consumer complaints was about specific transactions, transfers and payments. Among complaints received by ADR schemes and supervisory authorities, the second most common subject of consumer complaint was scams and frauds followed by complaints regarding fees and charges or poor value for money. Scams and frauds were less commonly the subject of complaints lodged directly with firms.

Table 6.1 presents data on the average change in the number of consumer complaints in the banking and payments sector between 2020 and 2022, split by the recipient of the complaint. Notably, the volume of complaints increased in both years and across all three recipients (firms, ADR schemes and supervisory authorities).

Table 6.1. Average change in number of consumer complaints in the banking and payments sector, by recipient of complaint

	Firms	ADR	Supervisory authorities
2020 to 2021	↑ 7%	↑ 18%	↑ 24%
2021 to 2022	↑ 18%	↑ 45%	↑ 9%
Number of reporting jurisdictions	15	12	25

6.3. Credit

Figure 6.3. Top five subjects of consumer complaints in the credit sector, by recipient of complaint

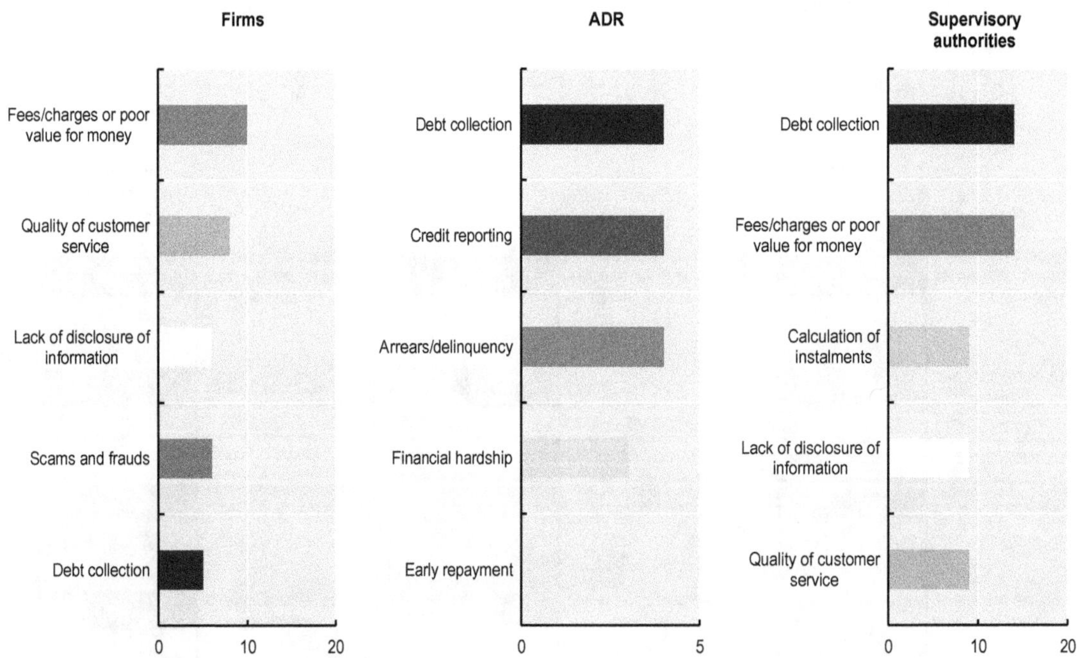

Note: Horizontal bars correspond to the number of respondents who ranked this subject of complaints among the top five in their jurisdiction in 2022.
Source: OECD Consumer Finance Risk Monitor Reporting Template 2023.

As shown in Figure 6.3, debt collection was among the top subjects of complaints received by ADR schemes and supervisory authorities in the credit sector. Fees/charges and poor value for money ranked as the top subject of consumer complaints received by firms and was tied with debt collection among complaints received by supervisory authorities. Quality of customer service ranked second among complaints to firms. Jurisdictions submitted the following subjects under the "Other" category: interest charges, disputes regarding individual transactions and outstanding amounts, credit approval and credit limit issues as well as debt restructuring.

Table 6.2 presents trends in the number of consumer complaints in the credit sector between 2020 and 2022, by recipient of complaint. The number of complaints to firms decreased marginally in 2021, and again in 2022. Complaints to ADR schemes grew slightly in both years, while complaints to supervisory authorities decreased overall.

Table 6.2. Average change in number of consumer complaints in the credit sector, by recipient of complaint

	Firms	ADR	Supervisory authorities
2020 to 2021	↓ 3%	↑ 6%	↓ 2%
2021 to 2022	↓ 5%	↑ 7%	↓ 13%
Number of reporting jurisdictions	14	10	23

6.4. Insurance

Figure 6.4. Top five subjects of consumer complaints in the insurance sector, by recipient of complaint

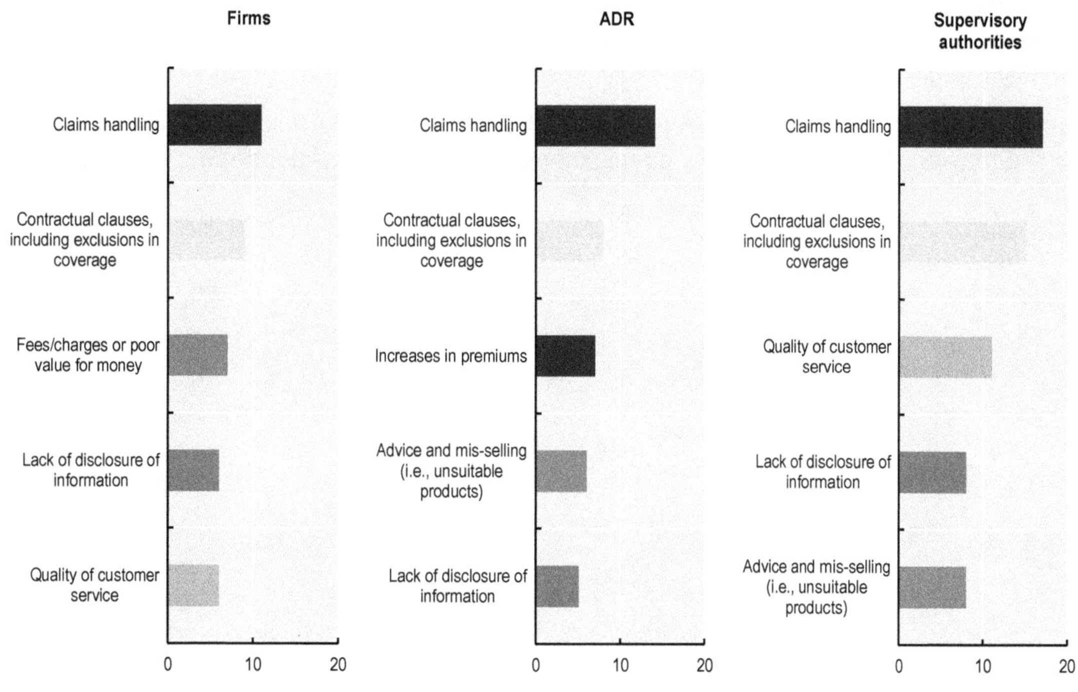

Note: Horizontal bars correspond to the number of respondents who ranked this subject of complaints among the top five in their jurisdiction in 2022.
Source: OECD Consumer Finance Risk Monitor Reporting Template 2023.

As shown in Figure 6.4, the top two subjects of consumer complaints across firms, ADR schemes and supervisory authorities in the insurance sector were claims handling and contractual clauses (including exclusions). It should be noted that complaints from consumers may be characterised as related to "claims handling" once their claim is denied – but the underlying problem may not stem from the claims handling process itself. Instead, it could result from poor product design, low value for money, poor target marketing mis-selling, among other reasons. Quality of customer service ranked third for complaints to supervisory authorities. Complaints related to claims handling involved claim amount issues (including disagreements about the valuation of damages), delays in claims handling and rejection of claims. Consumers also filed complaints related to underwriting practices, creditor insurance, product features and lapsing of policies (e.g. a claim is denied because the insurer claims the policy has lapsed).

Table 6.3 sets out trends in the number of consumer complaints in the insurance sector between 2020 and 2022. In general, the number of complaints fell over the time period, except for complaints to ADR schemes and supervisory authorities in 2021, which grew by 19 and 7% respectively.

Table 6.3. Average change in number of consumer complaints in the insurance sector, by recipient of complaint

	Firms	ADR	Supervisory authorities
2020 to 2021	↓ 5%	↑ 19%	↑ 7%
2021 to 2022	↓ 3%	↓ 7%	↓ 8%
Number of reporting jurisdictions	14	13	17

6.5. Investments

As shown in Figure 6.5, the top subjects of consumer complaints to firms in the investment sector were problems managing investments, problems related to fund withdrawals and advice and mis-selling. The most common complaints filed with ADR schemes and supervisory authorities related to advice and mis-selling and lack of disclosure of information.

Other complaint categories included the execution of orders, failure to follow instructions, unlicensed activities and market misconduct (i.e. alleged market manipulation and insider dealing).

Figure 6.5. Top five subjects of consumer complaints in the investments sector, by recipient of complaint

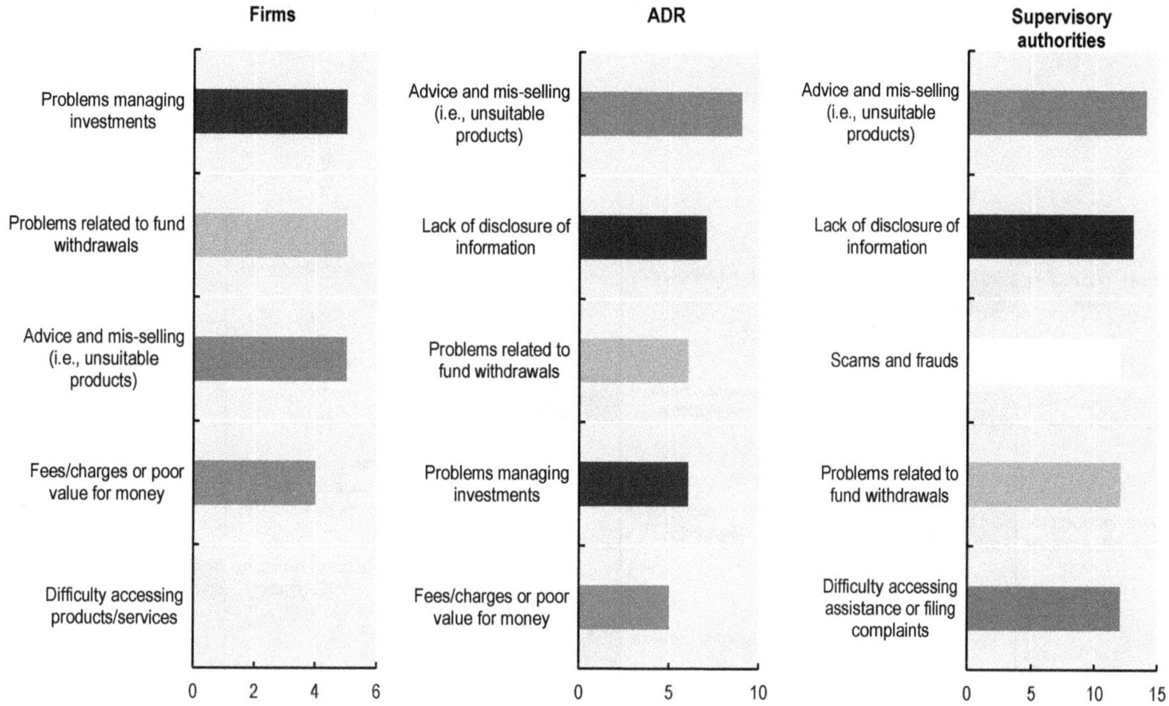

Note: Horizontal bars correspond to the number of respondents who ranked this subject of complaints among the top five in their jurisdiction in 2022.
Source: OECD Consumer Finance Risk Monitor Reporting Template 2023.

Table 6.4 shows average changes in the number of consumer complaints in the insurance sector between 2020 and 2022. The number of complaints received by firms increased in both years while the number of complaints received by ADR schemes fell. Complaints received by supervisory authorities increased overall, despite a small decrease in 2022.

Table 6.4. Average change in number of consumer complaints in the investments sector, by recipient of complaint

	Firms	ADR	Supervisory authorities
2020 to 2021	↑ 15%	↓ 4%	↑ 17%
2021 to 2022	↑ 62%	↓ 10%	↓ 2%
Number of reporting jurisdictions	12	11	21

6.6. Pensions

As shown in Figure 6.6, quality of customer service, fees/charges and advice were the top subjects of consumer complaints to firms in the pensions sector.[1] Complaints to ADR schemes and supervisory authorities frequently concerned fund withdrawals. Other complaints included contribution-related disputes and account administration errors, enrolment issues, transferring retirement funds, retirement annuities, delays in claims handling/ management and contract termination conditions. In addition, certain consumers in **Romania** had requests for information on the mandatory pension fund to which they had been randomly allocated. In **Mauritius**, the Financial Services Commission received complaints from private pension scheme members that they were receiving contradictory information from different insurance companies with respect to benefit payments; the Financial Services Commission conducted research on this matter and referred one insurance company in breach of the law to the enforcement directorate.

Figure 6.6. Top five subjects of consumer complaints in the pensions sector, by recipient of complaint

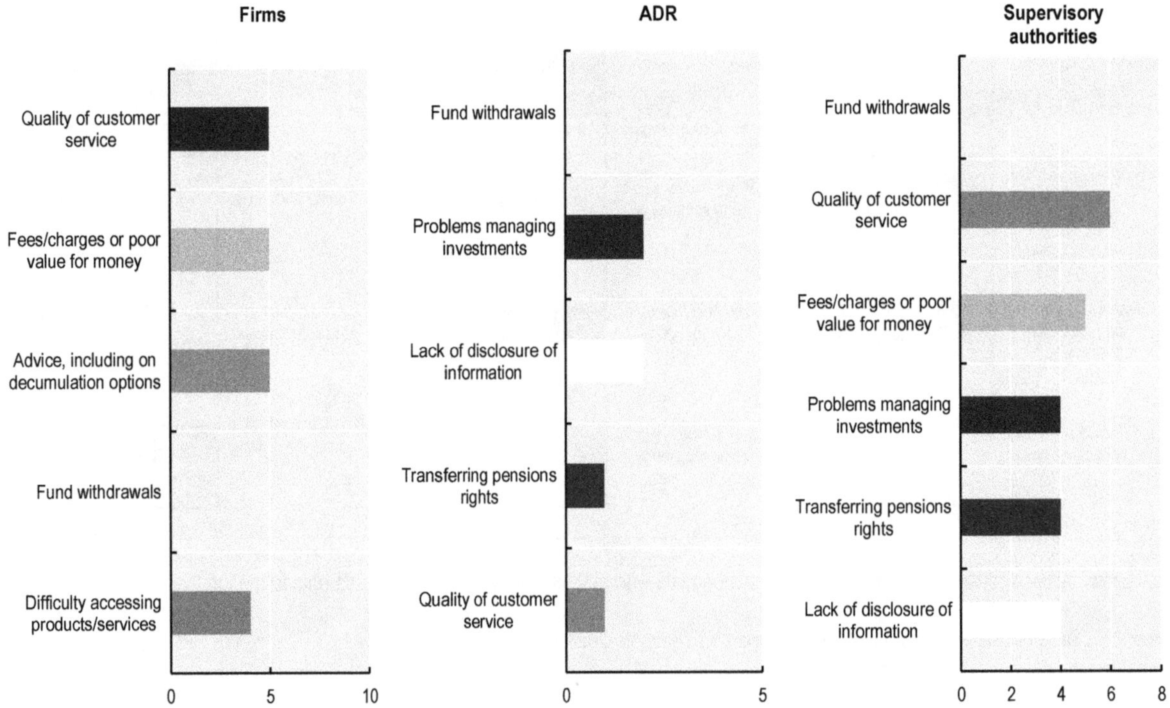

Note: Horizontal bars correspond to the number of respondents who ranked this subject of complaints among the top five in their jurisdiction in 2022.
Source: OECD Consumer Finance Risk Monitor Reporting Template 2023.

References

CGAP (2022), *Market Monitoring Toolkit: Analysis of Complaints Data*, https://www.cgap.org/research/publication/market-monitoring-tool-analysis-complaints-data. [1]

Note

[1] Too few responses were provided via the reporting template to be able to calculate a sufficiently representative average change in the number of complaints in the pensions sector, by recipient of complaint. Thus, the table that appears in prior sections of this chapter was not reproduced for this section on the pensions sector.

7 Financial scams and frauds

Financial scams and frauds rose in many jurisdictions during the COVID-19 pandemic, accelerated by increased remote access and widespread adoption of digital products and services. Financial scams and frauds continue to be a major cause of concern among jurisdictions. This chapter reports the most common financial scams and frauds in 2022. It also describes regulatory and supervisory actions taken to address the increasing incidence and complexity of financial scams and frauds.

While scams and frauds have always existed as a potential threat to financial consumers, in recent years their incidence has increased in many jurisdictions. Financial scams and frauds rose in numerous jurisdictions during the pandemic, accelerated by increased remote access and widespread adoption of digital products and services. Prior work undertaken by the Task Force during the height of the pandemic in 2021 gathered the views of 164 organisations from 81 jurisdictions on the impact of the pandemic on financial consumers; respondents identified vulnerability to scams and frauds as the second most significant risk for financial consumers arising from the COVID-19 pandemic (the top ranked risk overall was reduced financial resilience). Among responses from high-income jurisdictions, scams and fraud was the top-ranked risk (OECD, 2021[1]). More than 80% of respondents to the 2021 survey reported that the incidence of scams and frauds had increased since the start of the pandemic in their jurisdictions. The number of cross-border fraud complaints filed with econsumer.gov increased 257% between 2019 and 2020.[1]

As noted in Chapter 2, financial scams and frauds continue to be a major cause of concern for jurisdictions in 2022; among risks stemming from the operating environment, financial scams and frauds ranked second highest, after inflation and rising interest rates.

- As shown in Figure 7.1, most responding jurisdictions (72%) noted that the reported incidence of financial scams and frauds increased in 2022 compared to 2021. In **Singapore**, for example, the total number of investment scam cases increased by 26% from 2021 to 2022. In **Peru**, the number of unrecognised operations by credit and debit card users jumped by 19% in 2022.
- Conversely, the number of reported financial scams and frauds stayed the same in 7% of jurisdictions and decreased in around 21%.

Figure 7.1. Change in the number of reported financial scams and frauds, 2021 to 2022

Percentage of jurisdictions who reported an increase, decrease or consistent level of scams and frauds

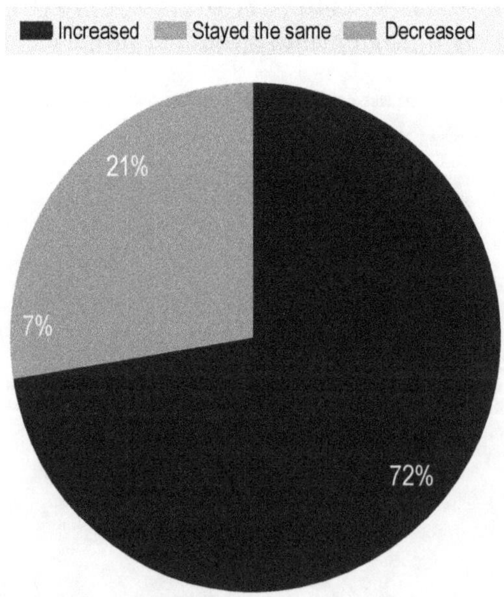

Note: Based on responses from 29 jurisdictions.
Source: OECD Consumer Finance Risk Monitor Reporting Template 2023.

In terms of the amount of financial losses due to scams in frauds, in the ten jurisdictions where data is available, the total amount of financial losses increased from 2021 to 2022. These increases in financial losses averaged 27%, ranging from a 5% increase in **Singapore** to a 79% increase in **Australia**.

- In **Israel**, the total amount of financial losses increased by around 7.5%.
- In **Romania**, the total amount of financial losses for payment service users increased by around 8%.
- In **Austria,** the total amount of financial losses due to scams and frauds increased by 17%.
- In **Malaysia** and **New Zealand,** the total amount of financial losses increased by 19%.
- In **Poland,** the total amount of financial losses increased by 32%.
- In **Chile**, the total amount of financial losses increased by 34%.
- In **Canada**, the total amount of financial losses increased by 37%.

As shown in Figure 7.2, the top types of scams and frauds by number of people affected were tricking consumers into providing personally identifiable information (selected by 86% of respondents) and fake schemes designed to tempt consumer to transfer, pay or invest money or buy fake insurance (selected by 84%).[2] Further details and examples of various scam and fraud typologies are set out in Box 7.1.

Figure 7.2. Top types of financial scams and frauds, by number of people affected

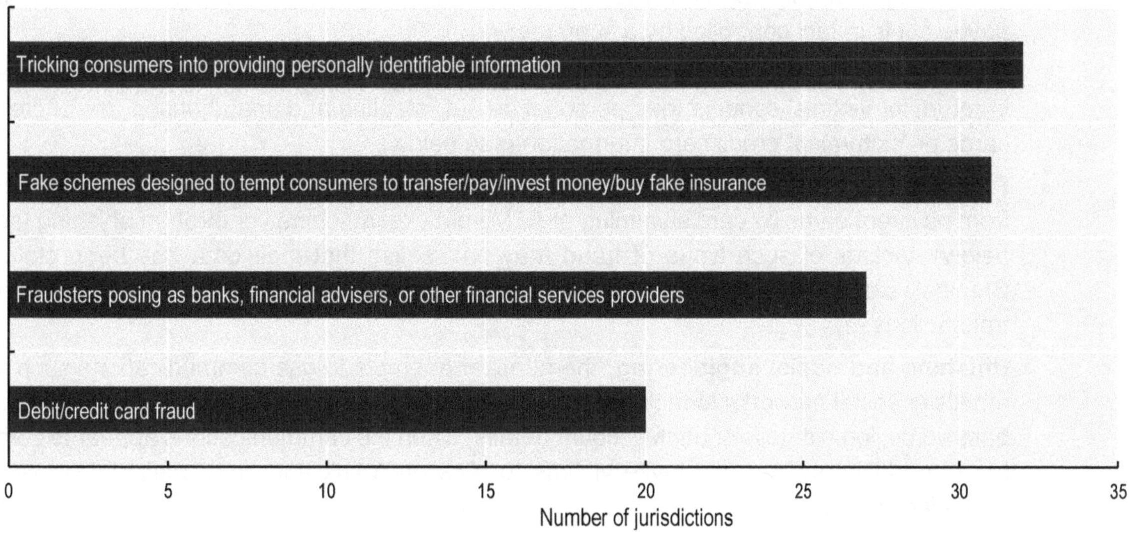

Note: Horizontal bars correspond to the number of respondents who ranked this type of financial scam or fraud among the top five in their jurisdiction in 2022 in terms of the number of people affected.
Source: OECD Consumer Finance Risk Monitor Reporting Template 2023.

The next-most selected types of scams and frauds in terms of the number of people affected and the total amount of financial losses include:

- mobile banking/digital wallet fraud
- identify theft
- fraudsters posing as representatives of the government, official entities or other organisations
- cyberattacks targeting customers
- fraudulent issuance of crypto assets
- SIM swapping.

The following types of financial scams and frauds were selected by two or fewer jurisdictions as the most significant types of fraud:

- cheque fraud
- selling fake insurance policies
- internal fraud
- skimming.

Box 7.1. Common financial scams and frauds typologies

Common types of online frauds and scams targeting financial consumers include:

- **Advance fee frauds:** these frauds have various different forms, but they all involve an email or other communication inviting the victim to pay money in return for receiving something of greater value such as a prize, inheritance, investment or transferred money. Advanced fee frauds include lottery scams, charity scams, impersonation scams, unexpected inheritance scams, dating and romance scams.
- **Authorised push payment fraud:** these scams occur when consumers are tricked into authorising a transfer of money to an account that they believe belongs to a legitimate payee but is in fact controlled by a scammer.
- **Bank loan or credit card scams:** these scams take the form of fraudulent bank loan offers in return for victims' sending their personal details, stealing and unauthorised use of credit cards or "skimming" credit card information (see below).
- **Payment card fraud:** in addition to lost or stolen card fraud, criminals may capture data from payment cards by card skimming at ATMs or ticket machines or through phishing (see below). Victims of such types of fraud may not realise that their data has been stolen. Criminals can use this data to create fake cards or to carry out fraudulent Card-Not-Present transactions.
- **Phishing and social engineering:** the attacker attempts to use communications such as emails or social networks to trick consumers into providing valuable personal data such as passwords, login details or bank account details. Often the communications appear to come from an official source and invite victims to click on a link and enter their details via a fraudulent website.
- **Malware attacks:** victims click on a link or attachment that installs or executes malicious software on their computer allowing the perpetrator to steal personal details and commit fraudulent activities such as unauthorised transactions. Ransomware is a type of malware that blocks or limits access to a computer or file with a demand for a ransom be paid to the scammer for them to be unlocked.

Sources: OECD (2020[2]), *Financial Consumer Protection Policy Approaches in the Digital Age: Protecting Consumers' Assets, Data and Privacy*, www.oecd.org/finance/Financial-Consumer-Protection-Policy-Approaches-in-the-Digital-Age.pdf; Interpol (n.d.[3]), "Financial crime", https://www.interpol.int/en/Crimes/Financial-crime.

Many jurisdictions noted that the rise in consumers falling victim to financial scams and frauds has coincided with an increased use of mobile and digital financial services, in part due to the lasting behavioural effects of the pandemic which moved activities online. As the volume of transactions grew on online financial services platforms, the sector became an increasingly attractive target for criminals, with an attendant growth in frauds. Younger investors, who have entered the market through digital channels (mostly investment platforms and apps) seem to be keener to make investment decisions on their own, or to follow financial advice from self-proclaimed experts on the internet (i.e. "finfluencers"), which can make them more susceptible to scams and frauds.

The increasing digitalisation of the financial sector has not only led to a higher level of fraudulent activity, but it has also altered the types of scams most frequently perpetrated. In **Nigeria**, for example, financial scams and frauds are shifting from counterfeit card capabilities toward harder-to-identify online fraud schemes. In general, fraudulent activity is becoming much more sophisticated – both in terms of cyber-attacks that target financial institutions and consumer-targeting scams. **Israel**, for example, noted the increasing use of IVR (interactive voice response) to carry out scams over the phone. In the **United States**, fraudsters are leveraging the faster (e.g. real-time or near real-time) and streamlined payment capabilities of innovative peer-to-peer (P2P) payment solutions, which have become increasingly popular among consumers. Fraudsters are using ever more complex forms of social engineering, which can be highly complex and fact specific. This is evident in the rising share of complaints relating to unauthorised transactions, as noted by Bank of **Italy** among others.

Another popular form of fraud consists of the creation of websites through which financial activities are illegally provided, which is an easy and inexpensive way to reach a vast number of potential victims. In some cases, as described by **Luxembourg**, these fake websites are detailed copies of the actual sites of supervised entities. As highlighted by **Italy**, the use of social media platforms can also help lure consumers toward these fake platforms. In **Greece**, the majority of complaints received by the securities supervisor in 2022 were about unauthorised brokerage firms that targeted potential investors through cold calls and fake advertisements on social media networks. Criminals may also misrepresent themselves as employees of a regulatory authority, in some cases even offering to provide redress to victims of earlier scams. In 2022, **Austria** witnessed a dramatic increase in scammers claiming to be members of the Financial Markets Authority. The Financial Conduct Authority of the **United Kingdom** similarly noted that "FCA scams" (i.e. fraudsters pretending to be from the FCA) were among five scam types most commonly reported to the FCA.

In **Indonesia** and **Thailand**, authorities have observed fraudsters tricking victims into downloading malware (such as an .apk attachment on Android phones), which can then be used to remotely control the device to transfer money through the victim's mobile banking application. Authorities in Thailand also reported that scammers had developed fake mobile loan apps, which required potential borrowers to deposit money upfront to guarantee loan approval. Borrowers made the payment, and the fraudsters absconded with the money without delivering the promised loan.

7.1. Regulatory and supervisory actions

The prominence of financial scams and frauds on the agendas of policymakers and regulators has grown in response to their increasing incidence and severity. Jurisdictions reported responding to the increase in scams and frauds with a range of regulatory initiatives and supervisory actions:

- In **Peru**, enhanced authentication regulation came into force in 2022, which included both digital services' onboarding and strong authentication requirements beyond the use of two-factor authentication. This regulation, which upgraded the security framework established in 2009, also established that the financial institution is responsible for any transactions that are a) reported as not recognised by the consumer (or occurring after the consumer has reported the loss or theft of their credentials) and b) not approved by strong authentication processes.
- In **Japan**, in response to a rapid increase in the number of cases of fraudulent money transfers, which were suspected to be caused by phishing scams, the Japanese Financial Services Agency

(JFSA) requested financial institutions to strengthen their anti-phishing measures in September 2022.

- In **Greece**, the Hellenic Capital Market Commission (HCMC) as published a warning to investors against investment risks and online investment fraud. The Bank of Greece also published a statement on digital private currencies warning consumers of potential investment risks.
- In the **United Kingdom**, the Financial Conduct Authority have continued to influence search engines and social media firms to prevent scams and other illegal financial promotions from being promoted. As a result, the regulator noted a 100% reduction in illegal paid-for advertisements on Google and Bing.
- During 2022, the Banco de **Portugal** pursued administrative offense proceedings against payment services providers for lack of compliance with the obligation to apply strong authentication requirements to access payment accounts.
- In **Italy**, CONSOB published a warning in October 2022 calling the public's attention to the risks associated with investment proposals made through the internet and over the telephone that, by unduly leveraging the reputation of the Amazon brand, promised unrealistic profit opportunities related to the alleged purchase of shares in the Amazon company. CONSOB noted that this example was representative of an increasingly common type of scam through which unauthorised entities launch online advertising campaigns related to fake investments in well-known BigTech companies, football companies and cryptocurrencies. These fraudulent initiatives, which consumers can join by filling in online forms, are aimed at obtaining investors' money or their personal data.
- In **Hong Kong (China**) the Hong Kong Monetary Authority (HKMA) frequently engages with other stakeholders, such as the Hong Kong Police Force (HKPF) and Hong Kong Association of Banks (HKAB), to enhance the prevention and detection of scams and unauthorised financial activities. For instance, the HKMA participates in the Fraud and Money Laundering Intelligence Taskforce (FMLIT), which was established by the HKPF and includes the participation of 23 retail banks. Selected fraud cases are shared at FMLIT, helping banks identify over 19 000 previously unknown mule accounts, taking prompt action and also supporting law enforcement investigations. The HKMA has also shared good practices on fraud prevention and detection with the industry.
- In **Indonesia**, OKJ and Bank Indonesia are part of an Anti-Investment Scam Task Force (Satgas Waspada Investasi) that includes the National Police's Criminal Investigate Department and the Ministry of Communications and Informatics. A top priority of the Task Force is to track the total amount of financial losses from scams.
- In early 2022, the Central Bank of **Brazil** (BCB) created a working group to propose actions to address weaknesses and gaps against fraud and scams and requested information on transfer, payment and purchase transactions from 34 supervised entities. The purpose of the working group was to obtain a financial trailing of frauds, whereby the results would provide insights that would help the BCB improve its regulatory framework and help supervised entities improve their procedures for monitoring fraud and scams and defining typologies. Based on the evidence collected, the working group suggested the mandatory sharing of (attempted) fraud among financial institutions to prevent new frauds and interrupt actions in progress. Thus, the National Monetary Council (CMN) and the BCB enacted a Joint Resolution establishing that supervised entities must share certain information on financial fraud.

References

Interpol (n.d.), "Financial crime", https://www.interpol.int/en/Crimes/Financial-crime (accessed on 15 December 2023). [3]

OECD (2021), *G20/OECD Report on Lessons Learnt and Effective Approaches to Protect Consumers and Support Financial Inclusion in the Context of COVID-19*, OECD, Paris, https://www.oecd.org/daf/fin/financial-education/G20-OECD-report-on-financial-consumer-protection-and-financial-inclusion-in-the-context-of-covid-19.pdf (accessed on 25 August 2023). [1]

OECD (2020), *Financial Consumer Protection Policy Approaches in the Digital Age: Protecting Consumers' Assets, Data and Privacy*, OECD, Paris, https://www.oecd.org/finance/Financial-Consumer-Protection-Policy-Approaches-in-the-Digital-Age.pdf. [2]

Notes

[1] Econsumer.gov began in 2001 as an initiative of the International Consumer Protection and Enforcement Network (ICPEN), with support from the OECD. Consumer agencies from more than 65 countries support the project, which provides a platform to gather and share cross-border e-commerce complaints.

[2] Percentages are calculated based on the number of respondents who provided answers to this question (N=37).

8 Thematic risks and areas of concern, policy responses and next steps

This chapter reports on thematic risks and highlights responses that can contribute toward risk mitigation. The chapter also discusses next steps for policymakers, regulators and supervisors.

8.1. Thematic risks and areas of concerns

While the Monitor has addressed risks from different perspectives (including sectors, sources of risk, etc.), this final chapter aims to synthesise concerns across sectors and products to highlight thematic risks and areas of concerns that emerged from jurisdictions' responses to the reporting template.

8.1.1. Increasing incidence and complexity of scams and frauds

As the financial landscape evolves with increased remote access and increasing adoption of digital products and services, jurisdictions around the globe noted that financial scams and frauds were becoming more frequent and more complex. The majority of jurisdictions reported an increased incidence of scams and frauds in 2022. Even though financial scams have always loomed as a threat to consumers – even in analogue environments – jurisdictions agree that the increased use of mobile and digital services was accompanied by an attendant rise in scams and frauds. The greater use of digital tools has also affected the types of scams.

This trend threatens to undermine recent gains made in expanding access to financial services, as consumers may understandably withdraw from digital services that expose them to harm. It also damages the financial well-being of consumers and households, at a time when they are buffeted by various crises and threats, adding to overall vulnerability.

8.1.2. Emergence of new credit products and risk of over-indebtedness

Over the course of 2022, inflation and increases in interest rates all contributed to a cost-of-living crisis that put a strain on household finances around the world. In some jurisdictions, new credit products that had emerged in recent years (such as Buy Now Pay Later) offered consumers novel ways to manage their finances. However, jurisdictions are concerned that these same products could increase the risk of over-indebtedness among financial consumers, especially those experiencing acute financial hardship. Inadequate creditworthiness assessments and opaque fee schedules could lead to consumers taking on unsustainable debt and devoting too much of their income to unexpected fees and charges. Jurisdictions are also actively monitoring how interest rate hikes have affected households' overall debt burdens.

8.1.3. Innovation in digital technology and business models

Innovation in the financial sector can help widen opportunities for financial consumers and help drive financial inclusion. The rapid pace of innovation, however, could also lead to consumer harm. The Central Bank of **Nigeria** (CBN), for example, noted that digital financial services have exacerbated existing consumer risks and continued to introduce new and ever-evolving risks, given the dynamic nature of financial technology. CBN cautioned that these risks could undermine the delivery of digital financial services to underserved and low-income consumers and, if ignored, were likely to erode consumer trust in digital services.

Decentralised finance (DeFi), which uses distributed ledger/blockchain technology, as does crypto-assets, was cited by authorities in **Canada** and **Italy**, who highlighted how various firms have entered these spaces to act as intermediaries between DeFi and traditional financial markets, presenting new risks with potential implications for financial stability given the possible interconnections between DeFi and traditional markets (OECD, 2022[1]).

The use of artificial intelligence (AI) and machine learning has also emerged as a source of innovation and potential concern for authorities. While AI and machine learning has the potential to improve financial services, e.g. through risk assessments and personalised recommendations, these technologies also present potential risks, including through the perpetuation of biases and discrimination that already exist in financial systems (OECD, 2021[2]).

Firms are also innovating in terms of their business models, which can bring benefits to consumers but also introduce new risks. **Brazil** referenced risks arising from the emerging “Bank-as-a-Service” (BaaS) business model, including a lack of clarity over how responsibility is shared between regulated entities and the new providers contracting their services and the legal nature of the new providers (i.e. whether they are operating without required authorisation). **Malaysia** noted that evolving business models and rapid product innovation were outpacing regulatory developments and could result in lack of consumer protection and leave consumers vulnerable to unfair treatment. For example, an increasing trend of unregulated e-commerce providers partnering with insurers to distribute insurance products may heighten the risk of mis-selling or product pushing. Jurisdictions also described how digital innovation is coinciding with and, in some cases, accelerating the disappearance of physical bank branches.

8.1.4. Increasing access to crypto-assets

While not entirely novel, authorities continue to have concerns about crypto-assets. Their anonymity can facilitate fraud, according to respondents, and they are useful for facilitating money laundering. The lack of regulation over crypto-exchanges and/or noncompliance by crypto-exchanges with applicable domestic regulations was also cited as a risk factor. The involvement of regulated entities in crypto-asset-related activities was a concern from some authorities; one respondent noted that “financial services providers were eager to join the cryptocurrency craze despite its drastically volatile nature which made it inappropriate for the masses.” Research from the **United States** demonstrated that the crypto-asset-owning population is younger, more financially vulnerable and diverse than the general population. Research from the Competition and Consumer Protection Commission of **Ireland** similarly revealed that 25- to 34-year-olds were twice as likely as the general population to hold crypto-assets in some form.

Jurisdictions noted that crypto-assets have become significantly more accessible in recent years, despite their high risk and speculative nature. In **Luxembourg**, for example, more and more consumers are regularly exposed to promotion campaigns for “easy” investments in crypto-assets by user-friendly exchange programmes. Authorities in **Ireland** also noted the availability and ease of purchasing crypto-assets, which is a cause for concern given that the products are unregulated or in non-compliance with applicable regulations, and extremely volatile.

8.1.5. Alternative sources of financial advice (e.g. “finfluencers”)

Increasing access to crypto-assets, which may be unregulated in some jurisdictions or issued and/or traded in non-compliance with applicable domestic regulations in others, is related to another emerging trend concerning the confluence of a) self-directed investors, b) online “zero commission” trading platforms and c) financial influencers (i.e. “finfluencers”) who provide advice over social media, in some cases encouraging the purchase of virtual assets. As authorities in **Canada** reported, retail investor participation in capital markets saw rapid growth during the pandemic years, particularly in terms of self-directed investors. For some, the desire for returns in the face of challenging economic conditions may have led to more speculative investments, such as crypto-assets. Authorities in **Portugal** similarly noted that younger investors who have entered the market through digital channels (mostly investment platforms and apps) seem to be keener to make investment decisions on their own, or to follow financial advice from self-proclaimed experts on the internet.

Meanwhile, online influencers encourage their followers to make certain financial decisions, leading investors to allocate resources to products and services that may not be suitable for them. A 2023 study conducted by FINRA Investor Education Foundation and CFA Institute found that social media was the top information source for Generation Z investors in the United States, Canada and the United Kingdom

(FINRA Investor Education Foundation and CFA Institute, 2023[3]). **Slovak Republic** noted the significant impact of influencers, who often give misleading information or fail to provide risk warnings. The Monetary Authority of **Singapore** (MAS) cited misleading financial services advertisements posted on social media that highlight unsubstantiated high returns without mentioning any specific products. MAS noted that consumers may not know the identity of the person posting the advertisement and whether the person is licensed by MAS.

Authorities in **Brazil** are especially concerned by instances of "finfluencers" being hired by regulated entities without due transparency, leading consumers to take unnecessary and misinformed risks. Furthermore, due to a lack of in-depth knowledge about financial products and services pushed to their audience or even in bad faith, influencers can contribute to the spread of financial crimes and fraud, with significant financial losses. As noted in Section 5.4 in Chapter 5, a survey carried out in **Brazil** showed that three-quarters of surveyed investors (average of 32) began making investments based on information they received from YouTube channels and influencers. The CVM (Securities and Exchange Commission of Brazil) is closely monitoring this trend and is studying a possible regulation on the subject to bring more transparency to digital Influencers hired by regulated entities.

In a related development, a warning to consumers about the risks of crypto-assets, issued by the Central Bank of **Ireland** in March 2022, emphasised that people needed to be alert to the risks of misleading advertisements, particularly on social media, where influencers were being paid to advertise crypto-assets. Bank of **Spain** has also highlighted trends related to the increasing number of advertisements using novel means of communication, such as social media or digital banners, as well as new ways of advertising, for instance using influencers on social media such as TikTok, Instagram or Facebook. These new trends required the Bank of Spain to adapt its banking advertising regulation. New regulation was enacted in October 2020, requiring financial institutions to comply with specific rules depending on the media in which the advertisement is going to be broadcast.

International co-ordination on this subject may be particularly relevant, given the global reach of online social networks. Indeed, a 2022 Report by the International Organization of Securities Commissions (IOSCO) details policy and regulatory guidance to help supervisors and regulators address emerging risks from the rise of "finfluencers" and online marketing (International Organization of Securities Commissions, 2022[4]). Among the report's policy considerations, it notes that IOSCO members should mandate that firms take responsibility for the accuracy of information provided over social media channels, including through influencers. IOSCO members should also require the appropriate disclosure of information, including risks and conflicts of interest. In the European Union, the European Commission proposed a new package of measures in May 2023 related to retail investment; among other things, the proposals aim to address misleading marketing, including on social media (European Commission, 2023[5]).

8.1.6. Greenwashing and risks related to sustainable finance

As noted in Sections 4.2.1 and 4.5.1 in Chapter 4, authorities are concerned about risks related to ESG, sustainable finance and greenwashing. Authorities in **Canada** noted that while the interest of institutional and retail investors in ESG finance continues, reporting practices are still nascent. Securities regulators in Canada continue to focus on efforts that promote confidence in corporate disclosures, including advancing ESG disclosure standards and compliance monitoring that support informed decisions by investors and market participants. CONSOB reported that some product manufacturers in **Italy** have begun to assign "green" labels to certificates issued and offered to retail investors. The offering documents of such investments specify the pursuit of sustainability targets and the compliance with rules dictated by codes of conduct, which are published by trade associations in the absence of a specific legislation. The business segment is also developing quickly in **Germany**, where authorities are alert to possible consumer risks and detriment. Legal and practical aspects of the regulatory response are still subject to discussion and development in the country; therefore, closely monitoring the market for risk is necessary, at least initially.

Authorities in **Portugal** also recognised that the potential lack of knowledge of ESG financial instruments (among consumers and financial intermediaries), combined with incomparability of information could place investors at risk of potential detriment and possibly generate financial losses. In line with these concerns, the CMVM described plans to conduct more robust supervision on sustainable finance in the second half of 2023. In **Chile**, the Funds Supervision Department of the Financial Markets Commission developed a survey on ESG issues, which was incorporated into the department's risk matrix. The Financial Sector Supervisory Commission of **Luxembourg** similarly identified sustainable finance as a key topic in 2023 and beyond. In April 2023, the CSSF published its supervisory priorities in the area of sustainable finance (Commission de Surveillance du Secteur Financier, 2023[6]).

8.2. Responses to current and emerging risks

Jurisdictions have undertaken and planned a range of initiatives to address current and emerging risks. The following section highlights promising and effective approaches.

8.2.1. Implementing and improving comprehensive financial consumer protection frameworks

A key response to help protect financial consumers from potential detriment is to strengthen or implement a comprehensive policy framework for financial consumer protection. As the leading international standard for effective and comprehensive financial consumer protection frameworks, the G20/OECD High-Level Principles set out the components that jurisdictions should consider when first developing a financial consumer protection regulatory framework. They also offer a roadmap for jurisdictions with established frameworks to improve upon their existing policies and regulations. Jurisdictions that have yet to implement the Principles (or have only partially implemented them) should prioritise the full implementation of all 12 Principles.

Many authorities described plans to review or issue new regulations to strengthen financial consumer protection frameworks. **Indonesia** will issue new or enhanced regulations to improve several areas, including rights and obligations for consumers. **Nigeria** and **Portugal** will revise regulations regarding disclosure. Nigeria will review the Consumer Protection Regulation to incorporate detailed disclosures for digital products and services. Portugal will extend the array of payment services included in Banco de Portugal's Fees Comparison Website, to include instant credit transfers and operations performed through payment applications operated by third parties.

Building on its updated complaints-handling regulatory framework, **Peru** described plans to enhance market conduct requirements for digital financial products and services, introduce new rules for eliminating dark patterns and expand requirements in product design and distribution. **Finland** amended its Consumer Protection Act in early 2023 and thereby introduced stricter provisions on good lending and marketing practices, lower interest rate caps and stronger authentication requirements.

In **New Zealand**, the Conduct of Financial Institutions [Amendment] Act (CoFI) will become law in 2025. This will require deposit takers, banks and insurers to implement a fair conduct principle, which would mean: paying due regard to consumers' interests; acting ethically, transparently, and in good faith; assisting consumers to make informed decisions; ensuring the products and services the financial institution provides are likely to meet the requirements and objectives of likely consumers (when viewed as a group); and not subjecting consumers to unfair pressure or tactics, or undue influence.

Bank of **Thailand** cited plans to issue new regulation on Responsible Lending by the end of 2023, and in May 2023 the Government of **Australia** announced its intention to regulate Buy Now Pay Later products under the National Consumer Credit Protection Act (2009). In addition to the July 2023 introduction of the new Consumer Duty, which sets higher and clearer standards of consumer protection across financial services and requires firms to put their customers' needs first, the **United Kingdom** is also developing regulatory regimes for Buy Now Pay Later and crypto-assets.

In **Bulgaria**, the Bulgarian National Bank has introduced more detailed reporting of payments and fraud given the new Payments Statistics Regulation in Europe, which establishes new reporting requirements in relation to innovative payment services and channels, payment schemes and fraudulent payment transactions.

8.2.2. Strengthening supervisory capacity

Second, jurisdictions described a range of initiatives aimed at strengthening supervisory capacity, including new activities, investments and approaches.

National Bank of **Rwanda** cited mystery shopping, while Banco de **Moçambique** and **Brunei Darussalam** Central Bank described plans to develop their first risk-based frameworks for market conduct supervision. The Financial Markets Commission (CMF) of **Chile** noted work underway to define market conduct standards to be met by CMF's supervised institutions. Bank of **Spain** also noted intentions to develop and improve the implementation of a risk assessment framework focusing on conduct oversight, building on market conduct reporting requirements introduced in 2022. The FCAC in **Canada** created a dedicated supervisory team that will plan and conduct thematic reviews. OJK, the Financial Services Authority of **Indonesia**, is developing an internal task force to serve as a quick response team and investigate potential problems based on early warning signs.

In **Peru**, the Superintendency of Banking, Insurance and Private Pension Funds (SBS) described the process of implementing a transformational project to enhance their supervisory model and identify potential gaps in its regulatory framework. The enhanced model started with an internal reorganisation of SBS's market conduct supervision structure, which since 2022 has comprised three specialised departments and a general head. These departments supervise market conduct management as well as interest rates, analyse different sources of user complaints (including those posted on social networks), and apply corrective action. As a result of the reorganisation and the new functions assigned to the team, SBS increased the number of market conduct supervisors. In addition, SBS is improving their supervisory guides, building risk dashboards and exploring other SupTech tools to monitor conduct risks.

The Financial Sector Conduct Authority (FSCA) of **South Africa** similarly described plans to enhance supervisory engagement models (including at Board and senior leadership level) and increase the sophistication of supervisory models for assessing the fairness and nature of customer service in the banking system. FSCA also plans to enhance and refine conduct risk indicators to strengthen reporting and analytics on identified conduct risks across financial institutions. In **New Zealand**, regulatory Returns will be introduced in 2024 to provide additional insights into provider behaviour, while in **Spain**, the DGSFP (Dirección General de Seguros y Fondos de Pensiones) plans to develop and improve the implementation of a risk assessment framework focusing on conduct oversight.

...with a focus on culture

Three jurisdictions described a focus on culture as part of efforts to address conduct risks and improve outcomes for consumers.

- In **Australia**, the Government is establishing the Financial Accountability Regime (FAR) to improve the operating culture of entities in the banking, insurance and superannuation industries and to increase transparency and accountability across these industries. The FAR aims to deter poor behaviour and ensure that financial institutions and their senior executives are held to account when they fail to meet their obligations. The enforcement powers of the FAR are designed to combat serious regulatory issues such as prudential risk to the Australian financial system or significant and systemic consumer harms. Legislation to establish the FAR was reintroduced into Parliament in March 2023 and as of August 2023 remained subject to Parliamentary consideration.

- In **Hong Kong (China)** the Insurance Authority is building on its existing risk-based supervisory approach and focusing more on insurers' business conduct to ensure they have sufficient controls in place to get the basics right. As such, IA is allocating more supervisory attention to the insurers' governance culture and their control functions, including dedicating more resources to on-site inspections to insurers focusing on their business conduct and collecting additional data to assess culture.
- The FSCA of **South Africa** described similar plans to interrogate and assess the extent to which financial institutions have embedded good conduct in their cultures. Specific indicators and information gathering questions have been built into the new conduct returns to assist in measuring fair outcomes and assessing a firm's culture. Supervisors have also started attending operational meetings of the banks and insurers, (e.g. complaints handling meetings, product approval meetings and claims meetings) to observe firm culture.

8.2.3. Protecting consumers at heightened risk of vulnerability

As part of a comprehensive financial consumer protection framework, it is important to also protect consumers who may be at heightened risk of experiencing vulnerability.

While jurisdictions define vulnerability differently depending on the context, a general definition states that: vulnerable consumers are consumers who are "susceptible to detriment at a particular point in time, owing to the characteristics of the market for a particular product, the product's qualities, the nature of a transaction or the consumer's attributes or circumstances" [OECD/LEGAL/0403]. The wide range of contexts in which financial vulnerability can occur demonstrates how financial shocks can cause anyone to experience financial vulnerability, regardless of their prior circumstances.

One way to address consumers experiencing vulnerability is through access to consumer protection hardship arrangements. A key insight from jurisdiction's experiences with the COVID-19 pandemic was the importance of appropriate hardship arrangements for consumers experiencing financial difficulty. These hardship measures were most effective when implemented quickly and with a high degree of flexibility to provide short-term relief to mitigate the impact of emergency measures.

Given the challenging macroeconomic conditions in 2022, jurisdictions described targeted initiatives aimed at consumers who may be more likely to experience vulnerability or who are already in financial difficulty.

- The Securities Commission **Malaysia** described targeted outreach efforts to vulnerable populations, which include consumers who are living in rural areas, elderly, and those in a low-income bracket.
- Similarly in **Canada**, the Ontario Securities Commission reported plans to continue outreach focused on multicultural and diverse communities. Taking vulnerable customers into account is a subject of interest for all Canadian regulatory authorities, in the context of an aging population combined with the increase in the digital service offer and the associated risk of fraud. For example, data from the Autorité des marchés financiers (AMF) indicated that financial institutions in Québec met only 54% of the AMF's expectations in terms of taking into account the needs of vulnerable clients. Vulnerable clients have an increased risk of fraud and abuse caused in part by the decline of faculties (loss of memory, difficulty filling out forms, confusion, etc.). Canadian authorities are concerned that the current economic climate could result in greater fraud and criminal activity, as well as increased affordability issues, which would disproportionately affect vulnerable consumers.
- In **Colombia**, the Financial Superintendency (SFC) decided to develop a regional supervisory strategy consisting of traveling to municipalities far from the main cities to know how financial

consumers are treated and to evaluate the policies and guidelines that financial entities implement regarding fair treatment.

- In **Peru**, access to the financial system by immigrants and refugees is made complicated due to barriers related to the different types of ID involved (both permanent and temporary) and the lack of knowledge from financial institutions' personnel on how to validate those IDs for KYC purposes. As a result, in co-ordination with both national and international organisations, SBS published guidance on the financial inclusion of immigrants and refugees, which covers, among other things, the main ID documents used by this group and their characteristics and validation mechanisms (SBS et al., 2023[7]). SBS also launched a cycle of seminars with associations of financial institutions to disseminate the guidance and reduce this knowledge barrier among financial institutions.
- The National Bank of **Poland** referenced a "cash protection scheme" that ensures that digitally excluded (usually older) consumers can pay with cash whenever they like. In addition, many Ukrainian refugees were successfully integrated within Polish financial system, due to combined efforts of the public administration and the financial sector.
- The Bank of **Italy** described plans to focus on situations of customer distress and mitigating risks of over-indebtedness. The initial analysis will aim to increase the Bank's understanding of the procedures adopted by intermediaries for the prevention, detection and management of cases of consumers in financial difficulties. The Bank of Italy is committed to ensuring that debt collection procedures, which are often outsourced to third parties, duly take into account the situation of the consumer and are not overly invasive.
- In **France**, the Lemoine Law passed in 2022 reduced to five years the right for applicants formerly suffering from cancer, hepatitis C and other chronic disease not to declare their disease. It also abolished medical questionnaires for housing loans below EUR 200 000 and whose repayment due date falls before the borrower's 60th birthday.
- Regarding consumers who have already been the victims of harm, the Government of **Australia** is establishing a Compensation Scheme of Last Resort (CSLR) to support ongoing confidence in the financial services external dispute resolution framework. Subject to the passage of legislation, the CSLR would facilitate the provision of up to AUD 150 000 in compensation to eligible consumers who have suffered misconduct by their financial services provider as determined by the financial system dispute resolution ombudsman, the Australian Financial Complaints Authority (AFCA).

8.2.4. Empowering financial consumers

… with digital tools

Another channel through which authorities can complement financial consumer protection policies is by promoting consumer empowerment. To reach this goal, jurisdictions described the use of price comparison tools, calculators and certifications aimed at consumers to help them make informed financial decisions and support healthy competition in the market. In **Poland**, the Consumer Protection Office developed an online mortgage calculator, which allowed consumers to check how payments would change with the rise of interest rates and how much they could save on interest with early repayments. The introduction of this tool was very timely, and it quickly became popular among online users. National Bank of **Rwanda** also launched a price comparison tool that aggregates information on interest rates and tariffs on loans, deposit accounts, cards and e-banking. The Central Bank of **Hungary** (MNB) referenced two consumer-facing platforms that aim to support transparency, comparability, public awareness and through this product innovation. First, a Consumer-Friendly certification framework that accounts for competitiveness, financial stability and consumer protection is available for three product types: housing loans, home insurance and personal loans. The MNB operates an online comparison site that allows consumers to compare such products in a standardised, easily comparable and transparent way, providing them with information on the main parameters of the products offered by the institutions. Second, a Green Financial Product Finder was launched in April 2023 focusing on green investment funds, green unit-linked life insurance and green voluntary pension funds. The Competition and Consumer Protection Commission of **Ireland** similarly runs public awareness campaigns to encourage consumers to use their comparison tools and calculators to see how much money they can save by switching financial products.

... and through financial literacy

Another strategy that can complement financial consumer protection is to support consumers' capabilities to make informed financial decisions by improving financial literacy levels in line with the OECD Recommendation on Financial Literacy (OECD, 2022[8]) . Many jurisdictions aim to improve consumers' financial literacy through financial education and/or public awareness campaigns. **Ireland** has carried out market research and PR campaigns to inform and educate consumers, particularly young consumers ages 18-35, on BNPL and crypto-assets. To help consumers better understand investment risks linked to crypto-assets, Bank of **Greece** issued a Q&A on bitcoin on its website. **Nigeria** introduced a new e-learning platform. **Ontario (Canada)** redeveloped the OSC's investor website "GetSmarterAboutMoney.ca". **Germany** is working on a national financial literacy strategy and plans to launch a central platform for financial literacy in 2024. In addition, **Germany** also plans to develop a finance-themed board game as part of its strategy to improve financial literacy levels. The Financial Supervision Commission of **Bulgaria** launched an innovative mobile app for filling complaints in real time, which improved consumer awareness. Promoting financial literacy has been a top priority for the Banco de Portugal, which has its own financial education initiatives and also co-ordinates the Portuguese National Plan for Financial Education together with other financial supervisors. Financial education initiatives in **Portugal** include reaching target audiences through digital channels and e-learning platforms, as well as hosting training sessions and developing financial education materials.

8.3. Next steps

The Monitor describes how financial consumers are exposed to risk and underlines the need for appropriate mechanisms to address information and market power asymmetries that can lead to consumer detriment. Findings in this report also support the importance of holistic and comprehensive financial consumer protection frameworks to respond to such risks and minimise harm. In combination with the G20/OECD High-Level Principles on Financial Consumer Protection, the Monitor can also provide a useful template for country reviews of financial consumer protection policies and to identify areas that require additional scrutiny.

At the outset of this initiative, the objectives for the Monitor were to:

1. identify and track trends over time
2. assist with prioritisation; and
3. elevate the perspective of financial consumer protection policymakers and authorities in international policy debates by contributing to the available evidence base.

In line with these objectives, the next steps building from this publication include the following:

- Draw upon the findings to inform the Programme of Work for the G20/OECD Task Force on Financial Consumer Protection, including future areas of research, subjects of roundtable discussions and seminars, and the development of policy guidance.

- Disseminate the Monitor and its findings to policymakers, public authorities and other stakeholders who can draw upon it to inform law and regulatory reform to enhance financial consumer protection where required, guide market monitoring and effectively address consumer detriment.
- Evaluate the reporting template and data collection process to identify areas for improvement, with an eye toward future iterations of the Monitor and any lessons for responding jurisdictions regarding their data collection capabilities.

References

Commission de Surveillance du Secteur Financier (2023), *The CSSF's supervisory priorities in the area of sustainable finance*, https://www.cssf.lu/en/2023/04/the-cssfs-supervisory-priorities-in-the-area-of-sustainable-finance/ (accessed on 23 August 2023). [6]

European Commission (2023), *Retail investment strategy*, https://finance.ec.europa.eu/publications/retail-investment-strategy_en (accessed on 20 September 2023). [5]

FINRA Investor Education Foundation and CFA Institute (2023), *Gen Z and Investing: Social Media, Crypto, FOMO, and Family*, https://www.finrafoundation.org/sites/finrafoundation/files/Gen-Z-and-Investing.pdf (accessed on 20 September 2023). [3]

International Organization of Securities Commissions (2022), "Report on Retail Distribution and Digitalisation", https://www.iosco.org/library/pubdocs/pdf/IOSCOPD715.pdf (accessed on 25 August 2023). [4]

OECD (2022), "Institutionalisation of crypto-assets and DeFi–TradFi interconnectedness", *OECD Business and Finance Policy Papers*, No. 01, OECD Publishing, Paris, https://doi.org/10.1787/5d9dddbe-en. [1]

OECD (2022), "Recommendation of the Council on Financial Literacy", *OECD Legal Instruments*, OECD/LEGAL/0449, OECD, Paris, https://legalinstruments.oecd.org/en/instruments/OECD-LEGAL-0449. [8]

OECD (2021), *Artificial Intelligence, Machine Learning and Big Data in Finance: Opportunities, Challenges and Implications for Policymakers*, OECD, Paris, https://www.oecd.org/finance/financial-markets/Artificial-intelligence-machine-learning-big-data-in-finance.pdf (accessed on 21 November 2023). [2]

SBS et al. (2023), *Guía Práctica para la Inclusión Financiera de Población Fefugiada y Migrante*, https://www.sbs.gob.pe/Portals/3/jer/Materiales_EF/2023/GuiaPracticaPoblacionRefugiadaMigranteDigital.pdf (accessed on 20 September 2023). [7]

Annex A. List of participating jurisdictions

Table A A.1. List of respondents

Jurisdiction	Organisation
Australia	Department of the Treasury Australian Securities and Investments Commission
Austria	Austrian Financial Market Authority Austrian Federal Ministry of Finance
Brazil	Banco Central do Brasil (BCB) Comissao de Valores Mobiliarios (Securities Commision) Superintendencia de Seguros Privados (Superintendency of Private Insurance)
Brunei Darussalam	Brunei Darussalam Central Bank
Bulgaria	Ministry of Finance
Canada	Financial Consumer Agency of Canada Department of Finance Canada Canadian Anti-Fraud Centre (CAFC) Autorité des marchés financiers (Québec) Financial Services Regulatory Authority (Ontario) Ontario Securities Commission
Chile	CMF (Financial Market Commission)
Colombia	Financial Superintendency of Colombia
Finland	Ministry of Finance
France	Autorité de contrôle prudentiel et de résolution (Prudential Supervision and Resolution Authority) Direction générale du Trésor (Treasury) Autorité des marchés financiers (Financial markets authority)
Germany	Bundesministerium der Finanzen (Ministry of Finance) BaFin (Federal Financial Supervisory Authority)
Greece	Bank of Greece Hellenic Capital Market Commission
Hong Kong (China)	Hong Kong Monetary Authority Insurance Authority Securities and Futures Commission Mandatory Provident Fund Schemes Authority
Hungary	Magyar Nemzeti Bank (Central bank)
Indonesia	Bank Indonesia OJK (Financial Services Authority)
Ireland	Department of Finance Central Bank of Ireland Financial Services and Pensions Ombudsman Competition and Consumer Protection Commission
Israel	Bank of Israel Israel Securities Authority Capital Market, Insurance and Savings Authority (CMISA)
Italy	Bank of Italy CONSOB (Securities Commission) IVASS (Institute for the Supervision of Insurance) COVIP (Supervisory Board on pension funds)
Japan	Financial Services Agency

Jurisdiction	Organisation
Lithuania	Bank of Lithuania
Luxembourg	Commission de Surveillance du Secteur Financier (Financial Sector Supervisory Commission) Commissariat aux Assurances (Insurance Commission)
Malaysia	Bank Negara Malaysia Securities Commission Malaysia
Mauritius	Bank of Mauritius Financial Services Commission
Mozambique	Banco de Mocambique
Myanmar	Financial Regulatory Department
The Netherlands	Authority for Financial Markets (AFM)
New Zealand	Financial Markets Authority
Nigeria	Central Bank of Nigeria
Peru	Superintendence of Banking, Insurance, and Private Pension Funds of Peru (SBS)
Poland	Office of Competition and Consumer Protection
Portugal	Banco de Portugal Comissão do Mercado de Valores Mobiliários - CMVM (Securities Market Commission)
Romania	National Bank of Romania Financial Services Authority
Rwanda	National Bank of Rwanda
Serbia	National Bank of Serbia
Singapore	Monetary Authority of Singapore
Slovak Republic	National Bank of the Slovak Republic Ministry of Finance of the Slovak Republic
Slovenia	Agencija za zavarovalni nadzor (Insurance Supervision Agency)
South Africa	Financial Sector Conduct Authority
Spain	Banco de España Dirección General de Seguros y Fondos de Pensiones (Directorate-General for Insurance and Pension Funds) National Securities Market Commission (CNMV) Secretaría General del Tesoro (Treasury)
Sweden	Finansinspektionen (Financial Supervisory Authority)
Thailand	Bank of Thailand
United Kingdom	Financial Conduct Authority
United States	Consumer Financial Protection Bureau Department of the Treasury Federal Reserve Board of Governors Office of the Comptroller of the Currency Securities and Exchange Commission

Annex B. Methodological notes for selected figures

Figure 2.1. Risks stemming from the operating environment

All respondents are represented in the graph. For full list, see Annex A.

Figure 3.1. Demand-side risks

All respondents are represented in the graph. For full list, see Annex A.

Figure 4.1. Conduct risks

All respondents are represented in the graph except Singapore. For full list, see Annex A.

Figure 4.2. Regulatory and supervisory actions taken in 2022 to address poor value financial products and services

Responding jurisdictions:

Brunei Darussalam	Ireland	Romania
Canada	Israel	Serbia
Finland	Japan	Slovak Republic
France	Lithuania	Slovenia
Germany	New Zealand	South Africa
Hungary	Peru	Spain
Indonesia	Portugal	United States

Figure 4.3. Regulatory and supervisory actions taken in 2022 to address the lack of or ineffective disclosures

Responding jurisdictions:

Australia	Ireland	Peru
Austria	Israel	Romania
Brazil	Italy	Rwanda
Brunei Darussalam	Mauritius	Slovenia
Canada	Mozambique	Spain
Finland	Myanmar	
Greece	Nigeria	

Figure 4.4. Regulatory and supervisory actions taken in 2022 to address poor advice and failure to perform suitability assessments

Responding jurisdictions:

Bulgaria	Ireland
Canada	Japan
Colombia	Mauritius
Finland	Mozambique
Greece	Myanmar
Hong Kong (China)	Portugal
Hungary	Rwanda

Figure 4.5. Regulatory and supervisory actions taken in 2022 to address unsuitable product design

Responding jurisdictions:

Australia	Nigeria
Brazil	Peru
Chile	Poland
France	Romania
Indonesia	South Africa
Luxembourg	Spain
Myanmar	

Figure 4.6. Tools used to monitor conduct risks

All respondents are represented in the graph. For full list, see Annex A.

Figure 4.7. Effectiveness of tools used to monitor conduct risks

All respondents are represented in the graph except Finland, Sweden, United Kingdom and United States. For full list, see Annex A.

Figure 5.1. Products and services giving rise to consumer detriment in the banking sector

All respondents are represented in the graph except the following. For full list, see Annex A.

Canada	Myanmar
Finland	Netherlands
Israel	New Zealand
Japan	Singapore
Luxembourg	Slovenia
Mauritius	South Africa

Figure 5.2. Products and services giving rise to consumer detriment in the credit sector

All respondents are represented in the graph except the following. For full list, see Annex A.

Brunei Darussalam	New Zealand
Canada	Nigeria
Greece	Romania
Japan	Singapore
Mauritius	Slovenia

Figure 5.4. Products and services giving rise to consumer detriment in the insurance sector

All respondents are represented in the graph except the following. For full list, see Annex A.

Finland	Nigeria
Indonesia	Portugal
Mauritius	Serbia
Mozambique	Singapore
Myanmar	Spain
Netherlands	Thailand
New Zealand	United States

Figure 5.5. Products and services giving rise to consumer detriment in the investments sector

All respondents are represented in the graph except the following. For full list, see Annex A.

Colombia	New Zealand
France	Nigeria
Germany	Rwanda
Luxembourg	Serbia
Malaysia	Singapore
Mozambique	Thailand
Myanmar	United States

Figure 5.6. Products and services giving rise to consumer detriment in the pensions sector

Responding jurisdictions:

Austria	Peru
Bulgaria	Rwanda
France	Slovenia
Hong Kong (China)	South Africa
Hungary	Spain

Israel	Sweden
Lithuania	United Kingdom
Mauritius	

Figure 6.1. Total volume of complaints

Responding jurisdictions:

Australia	Mozambique
Bulgaria	Myanmar
Canada	Nigeria
Chile	Poland
Colombia	Portugal
France	Romania
Hungary	Rwanda
Indonesia	Singapore
Israel	Slovak Republic
Lithuania	South Africa
Malaysia	Spain
Mauritius	United States

Figure 6.2. Top five subjects of consumer complaints in the banking and payments sector, by recipient of complaint

All respondents are represented in the graph except the following. For full list, see Annex A.

Brunei Darussalam	Mozambique
Colombia	Myanmar
Greece	Singapore
Japan	Slovenia
Mauritius	Sweden

Figure 6.3. Top five subjects of consumer complaints in the credit sector, by recipient of complaint

All respondents are represented in the graph except the following. For full list, see Annex A.

Brunei Darussalam	Rwanda
Greece	Singapore
Ireland	Slovenia
Japan	Sweden
Mauritius	United Kingdom
Romania	

Figure 6.4. Top five subjects of consumer complaints in the insurance sector, by recipient of complaint

All respondents are represented in the graph except the following. For full list, see Annex A.

Brunei Darussalam	Rwanda
Greece	Serbia
Japan	Singapore
Mauritius	Slovenia
Mozambique	Sweden
New Zealand	Thailand
Nigeria	United States
Portugal	

Figure 6.5. Top five subjects of consumer complaints in the investments sector, by recipient of complaint

All respondents are represented in the graph except the following. For full list, see Annex A.

Brunei Darussalam	Serbia
Japan	Singapore
Mozambique	Slovak Republic
Myanmar	Slovenia
New Zealand	South Africa
Nigeria	Sweden
Poland	Thailand
Rwanda	United States

Figure 6.6. Top five subjects of consumer complaints in the pensions sector, by recipient of complaint

Responding jurisdictions:

Australia	Israel
Austria	Italy
Bulgaria	Lithuania
Colombia	Mauritius
France	Peru
Germany	Romania
Hong Kong (China)	South Africa
Hungary	Spain
Ireland	United Kingdom

Figure 7.1. Change in the number of reported financial scams and frauds, 2021 to 2022

Responding jurisdictions:

Australia	Indonesia	Romania
Brazil	Israel	Rwanda
Bulgaria	Lithuania	Serbia
Canada	Luxembourg	Singapore
Colombia	Malaysia	Slovak Republic
Finland	Mauritius	Spain
Germany	Mozambique	Sweden
Greece	Nigeria	Thailand
Hong Kong (China)	Peru	United Kingdom
Hungary	Portugal	

Figure 7.2. Top types of financial scams and frauds, by number of people affected

Responding jurisdictions:

Australia	Indonesia	Poland
Austria	Ireland	Portugal
Brazil	Italy	Romania
Brunei Darussalam	Lithuania	Rwanda
Bulgaria	Luxembourg	Serbia
Canada	Malaysia	Singapore
Chile	Mauritius	Slovak Republic
Colombia	Mozambique	Spain
Finland	Myanmar	Sweden
France	The Netherlands	Thailand
Germany	New Zealand	United States
Greece	Nigeria	
Hungary	Peru	

Glossary

Term	Definition
Account information services	An online service to provide consolidated information on one or more payment accounts held by the payment service user with one or more payment service providers.
Agent fraud	Deceptive acts carried out by agents of a financial services provider against their customers.
Alternative dispute resolution mechanism	A generic term used to describe a range of procedures (including public ombudsmen or ombudsmen financed by relevant industry associations) designed to provide a way of resolving a dispute with a financial service provider (including their agents and outsourced parties) as an alternative to formal court procedures, and in addition to providers' internal complaints-handling mechanisms.
Buy Now Pay Later (BNPL)	A financial service, usually offered during the checkout process, that allows a customer to receive a good or service immediately but fully defer the payment for a certain amount of time or pay for it in instalments. The customer often, though not always, does not pay additional fees or interest charges if the instalments are repaid on time and in full. Generally, it involves a tri-partite transaction among the consumer, the merchant, and the BNPL provider.
Consumer complaints	Statements that express dissatisfaction or suspect misconduct by the provider of a financial product or service, including their agents and outsourced parties. Consumers may submit such statements directly to the provider, to a regulatory or supervisory authority, or to an external or alternative dispute resolution scheme.
Decumulation	The process of converting pensions or retirement savings into retirement income.
Digital wallet	Procedures agreed between the provider and the consumer to initiate payments from linked payment cards or accounts, which can be accessed through devices connected to the internet or through mobile communication systems. It can be incorporated in tools made available to the consumer by their financial institution or offered by a third party.
E-money	A monetary value stored electronically, including magnetically, represented by a claim on the issuer which is issued on receipt of funds for the purpose of making payment transactions, and which is accepted by a natural or legal person other than the electronic money issuer.
Financial scams and frauds	Deceptive acts or operations aiming to gain a dishonest advantage financially.
Gadget insurance	Policies that protect consumers' mobile phones or other electronic items against accident loss, damage or theft.
Innovation hub	Usually provides a specific scheme, via which firms can engage with the supervisor to raise questions and seek clarifications or non-binding guidance about FinTech related issues in the context of compliance with the regulatory framework, licencing or registration requirements, and regulatory and supervisory expectations.
Internal fraud	Deceptive acts or operations carried out by employees within a financial services provider.
Mobile banking	A service allowing customers to access their financial accounts, carry out transactions and manage their finances from their mobile devices.
Payday lending	Short-term, low-value, high-cost loans to cover immediate cash needs typically repayable on borrower's next payday or when income is received and usually granted without an assessment of the borrower's creditworthiness.
Price walking	A form of price discrimination, often in insurance markets, in which new customers are offered preferential rates while long-time customers see their premiums rise repeatedly due to factors that are not linked to the risk-profile of the customer and the cost of service.
Product governance	The systems, procedures and controls in place in financial services firms to design, approve, market and assess financial products through their life cycle to ensure that they meet consumers' interests and objectives and the relevant regulatory requirements.
Push payments	A payment transaction initiated by the payer or sending customer. In the context of PSD2, also known as "credit transfers".

Term	Definition
Regulatory sandbox	Provides a special scheme, in which companies can test innovative financial products, services, or business models with actual customers in a controlled environment (a 'sandbox') pursuant to a specific testing plan agreed with the supervisor and subject to the application of distinct safeguards.
Salary advance/earned wage access	A service, often offered by an employer in partnership with a third-party provider, that allows "early access" to a certain portion of an employee's wages before payday. Such services also exist under a "direct-to-consumer" form, in which providers gain access to a consumer's banking data and allow the consumer to request an advance on upcoming salary payments.
SIM swapping	A type of fraud that allows the perpetrator to gain access to the victim's phone number, which can then be used as part of two-factor authentications to access bank or other financial accounts. The scammer generally contacts the victim's mobile phone carrier and convinces them to activate a SIM card in the scammer's possession.
Super apps	Super apps provide end users with a one-stop shop for a variety of services (messaging, e-commerce, ride hailing, lodging – as well as payment and other financial services) and are typically offered by big tech companies, i.e. large companies with an established technology platform.
Supervisory letter	Official correspondence from a supervisory authority to a regulated firm. It can serve an educational purpose, i.e. to inform about the applicability of relevant legislation, rules, or guidelines and how they should be interpreted or applied in a specific situation. It may also serve as a warning, i.e. notifying a firm that they have violated a relevant rule under the supervisory authority's purview and that failure to remedy the violation may lead to enforcement action.
Supervisory statement	Guidelines issued by supervisory authorities setting flexible frameworks for firms, incorporating new and existing expectations.
Transaction account	An account at a bank or other financial institution that can be used to receive transfers, make withdrawals or initiate payments.
Unit-linked insurance	A type of investment, often offered by a life insurance company, in which the payments are linked to individual shares within a fund.
Warning/notice	A notice issued by a supervisory authority indicating its intention or consideration of taking further action against a regulated/supervised entity or individual.

www.ingramcontent.com/pod-product-compliance
Lightning Source LLC
Chambersburg PA
CBHW061222240926
51846CB00006B/1322